MW01075107

HOW TO
TALK
with
GOD

HOW TO **TALK** with **GOD**

JOYCE MEYER

Faith
Words

New York • Nashville

FaithWords
Hachette Book Group
1290 Avenue of the Americas, New York, NY 10104
faithwords.com
twitter.com/faithwords

First Edition: July 2023

FaithWords is a division of Hachette Book Group, Inc. The FaithWords name and logo are trademarks of Hachette Book Group, Inc.

The publisher is not responsible for websites (or their content) that are not owned by the publisher.

The Hachette Speakers Bureau provides a wide range of authors for speaking events. To find out more, go to www.hachettespeakersbureau.com or call (866) 376-6591.

FaithWords books may be purchased in bulk for business, educational, or promotional use. For information, please contact your local bookseller or the Hachette Book Group Special Markets Department at special.markets@hbgusa.com.

Library of Congress Cataloging-in-Publication Data
Names: Meyer, Joyce, 1943- author.
Title: How to talk with God / Joyce Meyer.
Description: First edition. | New York : FaithWords, 2023.
Identifiers: LCCN 2023003953 | ISBN 9781546016106 (hardcover)
Subjects: LCSH: Prayer--Christianity.
Classification: LCC BV210.3 .M494 2023 | DDC 248.3/2--dc23/eng/20230324
LC record available at https://lccn.loc.gov/2023003953

ISBNs: 978-1-5460-1610-6 (paper over board), 978-1-5460-0656-5 (ebook)

Printed in the United States of America

LSC-C

Printing 1, 2023

Contents

Introduction

Do you want to pray about something in your life, but you aren't sure how to do it? Or do you pray but wonder if God hears you? Do you believe your prayers are making a difference? When you finish praying, are you convinced that your prayers have accomplished something? Are you satisfied with your spiritual life, including your communication with God through prayer? Are you longing for a deeper, richer, more dynamic relationship with God through prayer?

Perhaps, as you read these questions, something inside of you says "Yes!" Over more than forty years of ministry, I have discovered that people really want to pray; they want to know that God hears their prayers and that their prayers are effective. People want to grow in their prayer lives and to see their prayers become more powerful as they pray for others and for themselves. There is nothing we can do on earth that is more powerful than prayer.

> *There is nothing we can do on earth that is*
> *more powerful than prayer.*

One of the most important, life-changing prayers any one person can ever speak is "Lord, teach me to pray." It's not just "Lord, teach me to *pray*," but "Lord, teach *me* to pray."

We need to learn how to pray as individuals with unique personalities, abilities, preferences, and gifts. God created each one of us specifically, and He wants an intimate, dynamic, personal relationship with us. Although certain principles of prayer apply to everyone, God leads each of us individually as we pray, and He wants to answer us in ways that are personal and meaningful to us. We make a mistake if we try to copy how someone else prays. I knew a woman who prayed from five to nine every morning, but when I tried that, I fell asleep. I had to find my rhythm in prayer, and so do you.

One of Jesus' disciples said to Him more than two thousand years ago, "Lord, teach us to pray" (Luke 11:1 AMP). Even though the disciples spent a great deal of up-close-and-personal time with Jesus, listening to Him, learning from Him, and watching Him work miracles, they still felt they needed Him to instruct them in prayer.

Years ago, I made that same request, and you can make it too. I said, "Lord, teach me to pray." God answered me in a powerful way and changed my spiritual life in wonderful ways. For example:

- I have moved from praying obligatory prayers or panic-based prayers to praying Spirit-filled, Spirit-led, faith-based prayers.
- I no longer focus primarily on prayers for my "outer life" (my circumstances, the activities I am involved in, the things that happen around me). I now pray for my inner life (the condition of my heart, my spiritual growth, my attitudes and motives). I also no longer pray merely for myself, but for many other people as well. As God has taught me to pray,

I have learned to pray to be strengthened internally and to ask Him to help me live out of a pure heart with right motives. God will take care of the externals. As I focus on Him, He will meet my needs.

- I used to strain and strive to manage five minutes of prayer a day. Now I enjoy it, and I actually need and want to begin my day with prayer. I pray throughout the day as the Holy Spirit brings people or situations to mind, finally ending my day communicating with God as I fall asleep. I like to pray my way through the day.
- I have moved from a sporadic, irregular prayer life to regular times of prayer that are disciplined without being legalistic.
- Where I once prayed to fulfill an obligation to God, I now realize that I absolutely cannot survive a day and be satisfied and content if I do not pray. I realize that prayer is a great privilege, not a duty.

Prayer is a great privilege, not a duty.

- I no longer approach God in fear, wondering if He will really hear me and send an answer to my prayers. I now approach Him boldly, as His Word teaches us to do in Hebrews 4:16, and with great joy and expectation.

I believe that if you will ask God to teach you to pray, too, you will also experience great changes in the way you pray, increased effectiveness in your prayers, tremendous satisfaction in your relationship with God, and a refreshing freedom and enjoyment in prayer.

I hope this book will serve as a "prayer primer" for people who may feel they do not know how to pray and as a refresher for those who may feel their spiritual life has become dry or stale. In the first part of the book, I'll help you understand that the basis for an easy, effective, enjoyable prayer life is your personal relationship with God and that prayer is probably much easier than you may think. In the second part, we'll look at several important habits of people who pray powerful prayers and several barriers to effective prayer. At the end of the book, I'll offer some closing words of advice and encouragement about how to stay strong in your prayer life.

I pray that regardless of your knowledge of prayer or your spiritual condition when you started, by the time you finish this book, you will be excited about prayer and feel equipped to pray with power, expecting God to answer.

God is the only one who can help you take the biblical principles you will learn in this book and cause them to spring to life so that prayer becomes exhilarating and effective for you. I am praying and believing that He will do that for you in an incredible, life-changing way. He knows exactly where you are on your spiritual journey, and He knows how to help you apply the teachings in the following pages in ways that will be just right for you, your personality, and the particular season you are in at this time in your life.

PART 1

Easy, Enjoyable, Effective Prayer

Chapter 1

You Can Enjoy Praying

I think most people would agree that effectiveness is important in prayer. We want our prayers to make a difference in some way. But have you ever considered prayer to be easy and enjoyable? I didn't see it this way for many years, but I have come to realize that prayer can be quite simple and still be powerful, and that I can enjoy doing it. And so can you.

Everything about our spiritual lives, including prayer, depends on our personal faith in God and our individual relationship with Him. We can enjoy that relationship because Jesus' death on the cross gives us free, unhindered access to our heavenly Father, and our faith makes it possible for us to have an intimate, dynamic relationship with Him. The more we enjoy our relationship with God, the more we enjoy prayer.

Ephesians 3:12 says that in Christ "we have boldness and confident access through faith in Him [that is, our faith gives us sufficient courage to freely and openly approach God through Christ]" (AMP). This scripture is exciting to me because it teaches us that as ordinary human beings we have *free access* to God at *any time* through prayer. We can approach Him boldly without reserve, without fear, and with complete freedom. How awesome is that?

> *The more we enjoy our relationship with God, the more we enjoy prayer.*

We don't need to try to sound super spiritual when we pray. We can be ourselves and be honest with God concerning our thoughts and feelings. The writers of the Psalms were totally honest with God about their feelings. The prayers we read there were not always polished and eloquent. Especially in the Psalms of David, we see that at times he poured out raw emotion due to the agony he felt as a result of his many enemies. Although he was brutally honest with God about how he felt, he always ended by telling God that he trusted Him and would wait on Him for His deliverance.

ASK JESUS TO TEACH YOU TO PRAY

Early in my prayer journey, I came across a wonderful little book that has helped millions of believers learn how to pray over the years. In this classic volume, titled *With Christ in the School of Prayer*, Andrew Murray (1828–1917) writes about asking God to teach us to pray: "None can teach like Jesus, none but Jesus; therefore we call on Him, 'Lord, teach us to pray.' A pupil needs a teacher, who knows his work, who has the gift of teaching, who in patience and love will descend to the pupil's needs. Blessed be God! Jesus is all this and much more...Jesus loves to teach us how to pray."[1] Don't just *try* to pray; ask Jesus to *teach* you to pray.

Jesus not only loves to teach *us*—corporately, as believers—how to pray; He also loves to work with us as individuals. He wants to take each of us just the way we are, wherever we are on our spiritual journey, and help us discover and develop a style of prayer that maximizes our personal relationship with Him. He wants prayer to be an easy, natural, life-giving way of communicating with Him as we share our hearts with Him and allow Him to share His heart with us. And He wants us to enjoy it.

Regardless of what some people may think, prayer is *so simple*. We'll look at this more in a later chapter, but for now let me just say that prayer is nothing more than talking with God. We speak to Him, and He speaks to us. God speaks to us in many ways. If you desire to learn more about *how* He speaks, I encourage you to read my book titled *How to Hear from God*.

God is far too creative to want every person on earth to interact with Him through prayer in exactly the same way. He is the one who designed us all differently and delights in our distinctiveness. There are principles of effective prayer that apply to all believers, but God leads each of us to pray as individuals. Just think of it: some people like to pray with music playing in the background; others like a quiet atmosphere. Some pray as they paint or draw; others like to make notes while they pray or write out their prayers. Some pray with their heads bowed and their eyes closed; others have their eyes wide open. Some speak to God silently in their hearts; others speak aloud. Some pray sitting in a certain chair; others pray while walking or on an exercise machine. As the saying goes, "Whatever works for you," as long as you are communing with God.

> *God leads each of us to pray*
> *as individuals.*

We are all in different places in our walk with God, we are all at different levels of spiritual maturity, and we all have had different types of experiences in prayer. As we learn to pray for the first time or as we grow in our prayer life, we need to move beyond intellectual knowledge about how to pray and take the information we read to the Lord and say, "Teach *me* to apply this in *my* life, in *my* situation, to *my* heart. Show me how this idea is supposed to work for *me*. God, I'm depending on You to teach me how to pray, to make me effective in prayer, to help me enjoy praying, and to make my relationship with You through prayer the richest, most rewarding aspect of my life."

YOU'RE FREE TO BE YOURSELF

Because we relate to God as individuals—and that's the way He wants it—we pray as individuals. Even when we pray corporately with others, we are all still individuals, and I believe that God wants our hearts to be in unity much more than He wants our methods to be the same. When we say, "Lord, teach me to pray," we are asking Him to teach us to pray in a distinctly personal way and to enable our prayers to be easy, natural expressions of who we are.

> *God wants our hearts to be in unity*
> *when we pray.*

We can feel free to be ourselves with God. We should go before Him just the way we are and give Him the pleasure of enjoying the company of the unique person He has made each one of us to be. We need to approach God with our own strengths, weaknesses, personalities, and everything else that so wonderfully distinguishes us from everyone else in the world. God enjoys meeting us where we are, developing a personal relationship with us, and helping us grow to become everything He wants us to be.

Psalm 33:15 says, "He fashions their hearts individually; He considers all their works" (NKJV). Because God has fashioned *your* heart individually, your prayers need to flow naturally out of your heart and be consistent with the way He has designed you. As you develop your individual style of communication with God, you may learn from people who are more experienced in prayer than you are, but don't make them your standard. There is nothing wrong with incorporating something someone else is doing into your prayer life if you truly feel God is leading you to do so. But don't force yourself to do what someone else is doing if you aren't comfortable with it in your heart. That wouldn't be enjoyable at all. In addition, don't try to keep up with others or copy their prayer styles or the length of time they pray, and do not feel compelled to use every prayer principle you have ever learned every time you pray. God's Word teaches us that we can pray anytime, anywhere, with all kinds of prayer.

When some people pray, they are more comfortable following specified rules or formulas for prayer than daring to follow the leading of God's Spirit. When we follow human-made rules, we please people. But when we step out in faith and follow God's Spirit, we please Him. We do not need to feel pressured to pray a certain way or for a certain length of time, or to use the words or phrases other people use. And we don't need to focus on specific topics in prayer because other people are doing so. We are free to express our uniqueness as we pray.

Some people feel safe when they are doing what everyone else is doing, but sadly, in the context of praying, they will also feel unfulfilled until they learn to untie the boat from the dock, so to speak, and let the ocean of God's Spirit take them wherever He wills. When we are in control, we know what will happen next, but when we let God's Spirit take the lead, we are in for a lot of surprises in life—and those surprises can be some of our most enjoyable, most thrilling experiences. We need to be determined to be ourselves and refuse to spend our lives feeling guilty because we are not like someone else.

> *When we let God's Spirit take the lead,*
> *we are in for a lot of surprises in life.*

My husband, Dave, has a passion to pray for the United States of America, and he does so on a regular basis. I have a passion to see God's children mature. I also have a great passion for the poor and oppressed, so I spend much of my prayer time praying about these situations. I know some people who focus intensely on social issues when they pray, and others who focus on missions with the same type of fervor. Some people pray passionately for their close family members or neighbors, while others pray just as passionately for people they have never met, such as government officials, celebrities, professional athletes, or little-known groups in undeveloped nations. My point is that God places different things on each of our hearts, and in this way, everything is covered.

No one can pray about everything that needs to be prayed about every day, but God's Spirit leads each of us if we allow Him to.

I suffered for a long time before I learned what I am sharing with you. At times, I found prayer to be laborious and even boring. I certainly didn't enjoy it, and I don't want that to happen to you. Let my pain be your gain. Start right now by asking Jesus to teach you as an individual how to pray in the unique way He has for you and to lead you to pray in ways you will enjoy.

Chapter 2

Talking with a Friend

The foundation of prayer is a personal relationship with God, and I believe effective, enjoyable prayer is based on being able to approach God as His friend, in addition to honoring Him as the almighty, all-powerful God that He is. Some people have a view of God that has never allowed them to consider seeing Him as a friend, but when we believe that God sees us as His friends and open our minds to the possibility of having Him as our friend, new wonders open up to us. God called Abraham His friend (Isaiah 41:8), and in John 15:15, while speaking to His disciples, Jesus said, "I no longer call you servants...Instead, I have called you friends." As a friend of God, we experience freedom, boldness, and increased confidence in God and His love for us, which are necessary for effective prayer.

If we do not know God as a friend, and if we

don't believe He thinks of us as His friends, we'll be reluctant to tell Him what we need or to ask Him for anything. If we have formal, impersonal, distant relationships with God, our prayers can be rigid and legalistic. But if we go to Him as our friend, without losing our awe of Him, our prayers will stay fresh, exciting, and intimate.

A natural friendship involves loving and being loved. It means knowing someone likes you, enjoys being with you, is on your side, wants to help you, cheers you on, and keeps your best interest in mind. A good friend is someone you value, a comrade, a partner, a confidant, someone who is dear to you, someone you want to spend time with, and someone you enjoy. You become someone's friend by investing time in them and with them, and by sharing your life with them. Saying that God is our friend is just another way of saying we have a close, intimate, personal relationship with Him, and it is not disrespectful. In fact, many scriptures speak of friendship with God (John 15:14; Exodus 33:11; John 16:13–15; Isaiah 41:8).

Developing your friendship with God is similar to developing a friendship with someone on earth. It takes time. You can be as close to God as you want to be; it all depends on the time you are willing to invest in your relationship with Him. The best way to get to know Him is to spend time in prayer and in His Word, the Bible. Your friendship with God will deepen and grow as you walk and talk with Him over time on a regular basis and as you experience His faithfulness in your life. The difference between developing a relationship with God as a friend and building relationships with people is that with God, you have a friend who is perfect— one who will never leave you, hurt you, or betray you, a friend who is faithful, dependable, loving, and forgiving.

The best way you could ever spend your time and energy would be to make a priority of developing a great holy friendship with God and inviting Him to be a vital part of everything you do, every day. This starts with simple prayer—just talking to Him and sharing your life with Him as you go about the things you have to do. Include Him in your thoughts, in your conversation, and in all your everyday activities. God is never more than a thought away. Just whispering "Father, I love You" is prayer. Talk to Him anytime, anywhere. Depending on your circumstances and surroundings, you may speak to Him silently in your heart or you may speak aloud, but know that He is *always* listening to you. Don't just run to Him when you are desperate; talk to Him in the grocery store, while you are driving your car, combing your hair, walking the dog, or cooking dinner. Approach Him often and simply refuse to do anything without Him. He really wants to be involved in your everyday life.

> *Just whispering "Father,*
> *I love You" is prayer.*

REMEMBER ABRAHAM?

Perhaps no one mentioned in the Bible is more often referred to as "God's friend" than Abraham (2 Chronicles 20:7; Isaiah 41:8; James 2:23). While the Bible refers to David in 1 Samuel 13:14 as "a man after His own heart" (*His* meaning God's) and to John as "the disciple whom Jesus loved" (John 21:7), Abraham has the distinct honor of being called the *friend* of God in more than one place in Scripture.

When God decided to judge the wickedness of the people of Sodom and Gomorrah, He told Abraham what He planned to do. We read about this in Genesis 18:17, which says, "Shall I hide from Abraham [My friend and servant] what I am going to do?" (AMPC). Why? Because they were friends.

In a friendship, people talk to each other about what they're going to do. How many times has a friend asked you, "What are you doing today?" and you replied with something like, "I'm going to the grocery store this morning and to a ballgame tonight." Or how often have you asked someone, "What's your schedule next week?" and they responded, "I have a doctor's appointment on Tuesday and a meeting on Thursday. But would you like to have lunch on Wednesday?"

Because God considered Abraham His friend, He told him what He was going to do—just like you would tell your friend. Proverbs 3:6 teaches us to acknowledge God in all of our ways. *To acknowledge* means "to own or notice with particular regard," which also means to care about what someone thinks. We should care about what God thinks of our plans, just as we care about what a close friend thinks. We should discuss everything with Him in a conversational manner, just as we would with a spouse or close friend.

When Abraham heard about the devastation God planned to release against Sodom and Gomorrah, he "came near and said, 'Would You also destroy the righteous with the wicked?'" (Genesis 18:23 NKJV). God had shared His intentions with Abraham because they were friends, and Abraham "came near" to God and respectfully questioned His intentions—because they were friends. They had a relationship in which they could talk openly and in which Abraham felt safe to ask questions. That's intimacy; that's confidence and security in a relationship.

The story is recorded in Genesis 18:17–33, but to summarize it, Abraham asked God to have mercy so the righteous people who lived there would not suffer the punishment due the wicked. After quite a bit of going back and forth, Abraham finally asked God to spare them for the sake of only ten righteous people—and God agreed. Why was Abraham able to intercede with such boldness? Because he knew God was his friend, and he appealed to Him on the basis of that relationship.

WHAT ABOUT YOU?

Just as God shared His plans with Abraham, He will share things with you—His heart, His desires, His purposes and intentions—when you are His friend. He will give you insight into what is happening in your life and tell you what to do about it. He may even let you know what is going to happen and how to prepare for it. He may not reveal everything you would like to know exactly when you would like to know it, but He will give you understanding and direction as you patiently trust Him.

You may be asking, "How do I get to be God's friend?" Jesus says you already are. In John 15:15, Jesus says to His disciples, "I have called you My friends" (AMPC). If you are a follower of Jesus, you are a modern-day disciple, and you are His friend. You can be a casual friend, or you can be a close, intimate, personal friend. It's up to you. Your friendship with God grows and develops just as your friendships with other people grow and develop. Just as a natural friendship requires time and energy to develop, so does your relationship with God.

> *Your relationship with God requires time and energy to develop.*

One of the best ways to ensure a deepening friendship with God is to have a heart that wants to obey Him. When our hearts are pure, tender toward His leading, and eager to respond obediently, we are in a terrific position to experience God's friendship. This doesn't mean we have to do everything right or try to be perfect all the time; it simply means we are not intentionally disobedient, rebellious, hard-hearted, or always trying to see what God will let us get away with. It means we are happy to put His desires before our own desires because we love Him and trust Him as our friend—and we know that what He wants is always best for us anyway.

As you grow in your friendship with God, never forget that your relationship is based on *who He is*, not on what He can do for you. Keep seeking Him for who He is, because focusing on the *benefits* of friendship with God instead of focusing on *Him* as our friend is a hindrance to a vibrant, maturing relationship with Him. The same thing is true in our relationships with people. We don't appreciate it when certain people want to be our friends because we have an ability to get them something they want. We feel valued when we know people want to be friends with us simply because of who we are and because they actually like us. Those are the relationships we most enjoy, and the same principle applies to our friendship with God.

I don't enjoy one-sided relationships in which I do all the giving and the other person does all of the taking, and I don't think God enjoys that either. You are free to ask God for anything, but don't forget to always ask what you can do for Him also. Many times, the best thing we can do for God is reach out to help one of His children.

One of the best ways you can spend your time and energy is by developing your friendship with God. Remember, Jesus has made you righteous through the blood He shed at the cross (2 Corinthians 5:21), so there is no reason you cannot approach God as boldly and as naturally as you would your best friend on earth. A growing, vibrant, increasingly intimate friendship with God will naturally lead to a growing, vibrant, increasingly effective prayer life.

Let me encourage you today to say this simple prayer: "Thank You, God, for extending Your friendship to me. Help me to be a good friend to You, and help me grow in my relationship with You as I learn to talk with You and hear Your voice through prayer."

Chapter 3

It's Easy

I believe prayer is not something we *have* to do; it's something we *get* to do. Prayer is the way we partner with God to see His plans and purposes come to pass in our lives and in the lives of those we love. It is the means by which we human beings on earth can actually enter into God's awesome presence. It allows us to share our hearts with Him, to listen for His voice, and to discover all the great things He has for us. Communicating with God is indeed the greatest privilege I can imagine, but this high and holy work is also the simplest privilege I know.

I don't think prayer was ever meant to be complicated. In fact, I believe that, from the very beginning of humanity, God intended it to be an easy, natural way of life by which people could stay connected with Him all day, every day. Jeanne Guyon wrote in *Experiencing the Depths of Jesus Christ* that "God demands nothing extraordinary. On the contrary, He is very pleased by a simple, childlike conduct. I would even put it this way: The highest spiritual attainments are really the ones that are the most easily reached. The things that are most important are the things that are the least difficult!"[2]

Prayer is actually much easier than most people think. In fact, Charles Spurgeon, who had a sophisticated theological mind, said succinctly, "When we pray, the simpler our prayers are the better."[3] God hears the simplest, faintest cry and receives the most childlike requests. I have raised four children, and I am now a grandmother—and I know that one thing children are *not* is complicated. They need to be encouraged to do things that are hard, but they will gladly do almost anything that is easy. They are not sophisticated enough to hide their hearts or feelings well, and as a result, communicating with them can be easy and refreshing.

We often say that children have no filters; they say exactly what they mean. As adults, we are not always wise to do this. We need to be prudent in what we say and when we say it. But when we pray, I believe that God wants us to be totally honest with Him. He knows everything about us anyway, so we are not telling Him anything that He doesn't already know. We are the ones who benefit by telling all. By doing this, we never feel that we have anything to hide. It is often said that our secrets make us sick, and I personally believe confession is good for us. God's Word teaches us to confess our sin in order to receive forgiveness, and the result is a type of cleansing of the soul (1 John 1:9). James even encourages us to confess our faults to one another that we may be healed and restored spiritually (James 5:16).

God wants us to be like children in many ways when we talk to Him. Just as little children are naturally inclined to trust their parents completely, we also need to be guileless, pure, and free from doubt as we trust God. When we pray with simple, childlike (not childish) faith, we can experience God's miracle-working power and see things change.

> *God wants us to be like children in many ways when we talk to Him.*

Years ago, God challenged me to try to ask Him for what I wanted and needed in as few words as possible. I had a bad habit of talking too much in prayer because I had the mistaken idea that short prayers were not good prayers. It is not the length of our prayers that makes them effective but the sincerity and faith behind them.

Let me make four observations about prayer that will hopefully help you see how easy it can be.

1. IT DOESN'T HAVE TO BE LONG

Perhaps the biggest misconception people have about prayer is that it must be long to be effective. It doesn't. There's no correlation between how long a person prays and whether God answers. The length of our prayers makes no difference to God. All that matters is that we pray the way He is teaching us to pray and that our prayers are Spirit-led, heartfelt, and accompanied by true faith. I have learned to pray until I feel full and satisfied in my spirit—and that takes longer on some days than it does on others. There is certainly nothing wrong with long prayers, and sometimes God leads us into extended times of prayer or even seasons of prayer. But I do not believe we need to labor to put in a certain number of hours in prayer, apart from the leading of the Holy Spirit, out of a sense of obligation.

When God challenged me to make my requests of Him in as few words as possible, He simply asked me to be concise and to the point and then to be quiet. When I did, I could not believe the increased power that came to my prayer life. To this day, when I pray that way, I sense more of the Holy Spirit's power and presence than I do if I go on and on and on and on. I have learned that some of the most powerful, effective prayers I can pray are things like "Thank You, Lord," "Oh, God, I need Your wisdom," "Give me strength to keep going, Lord," or "I love You, Jesus." And perhaps the most powerful of all: "Help!" See? Just a few words will connect us with heaven as we call upon the Lord to act on our behalf.

If God always wanted our prayers to be long and drawn out, I believe He would have put only long, drawn-out prayers in the Bible. But so many of the examples of prayer in Scripture are short and concise. In addition to that, Jesus said, "Do not heap up phrases (multiply words, repeating the same ones over and over)" (Matthew 6:7 AMPC).

If you have thought your prayers had to be long to be effective, I hope you have now been relieved of that burden. Just one word from a sincere heart spoken to God in faith and led by His Spirit can reach His heart and move His hand. When we approach prayer as an obligation and a work of our own flesh, five minutes can seem like an hour, but when our prayer is energized by the Holy Spirit, an hour can seem like five minutes.

2. IT DOESN'T HAVE TO BE COMPLICATED

Some people believe that prayer is complicated. Some have been taught they can only pray in certain places (such as a church building) or that they are supposed to pray at certain times. Some feel they need to use a specific formula or follow a model for prayer. Some believe prayer is difficult, that it has to follow a certain method or be spoken with certain points in a certain order, that we should only pray about certain things, that we better not overload God by asking for too much, that we have to be careful what we ask for, and that we have to fully understand God's will before we pray so that we won't pray outside of His will. We do need to pray according to God's will, but we should not become so nervous about it that we are afraid to ask God for the things that are on our hearts. The worst that can happen if we pray outside of God's will is that we won't get what we ask for—and that will be for our ultimate good. God knows our hearts, and He will not become angry if we make a mistake and ask for something that is not His will. We don't need to approach Him with the fear that we might make a mistake or that He will not be pleased if we ask for too much. Ephesians 3:20 states that He can do "exceedingly, abundantly" above and beyond all we can ever dare to hope, ask or think (NKJV). Perhaps instead of praying for too much, we pray for too little. We need to go to God in faith, boldly, confidently, and freely.

If we think too much about everything I mentioned in the previous paragraph, prayer *will* be complicated. But if we reject the ideas that complicate prayer for us, then we will find that it is not complicated at all. In fact, it is the easiest thing in the world and should come as naturally to us as breathing. As I mentioned previously, we can pray anytime, anywhere.

Another mistaken idea that complicates prayer

for some people and prevents them from praying is that prayer is only prayer when a person's eyes are closed, their hands are folded, and their head is bowed—or perhaps when they are on their knees. This could not be further from the truth. In fact, I think the best posture for prayer is one that is comfortable for you. If you aren't comfortable, you'll be distracted and unable to focus on God and enjoy praying.

Be free from everything you have heard about the formulas of prayer or the positions of prayer—and just pray. I challenge you to uncomplicate your prayers. Use simple words that plainly communicate your heart, reject any idea that prayer needs to be complicated, and begin to enjoy it as the simple privilege God intends it to be.

I challenge you to uncomplicate your prayers.

3. IT DOESN'T HAVE TO BE ELOQUENT

A major misconception about prayer is that people must use the "right words" and speak eloquently or with stilted language. I have literally heard people shift their entire vocabulary and way of speaking when they begin to pray. I don't know why, but some people actually speak in King James English when they pray, using words they would never use in everyday life. Unless you lived in the days of King James, such words would be out of character and uncomfortable for you.

God wants you to be comfortable with Him, so when you pray, talk to Him plainly and simply. If you are approaching God trying to sound eloquent, I urge you to just be yourself. The point I want to make is that prayer should be a natural extension and expression of your normal communication style. Prayer needs to be comfortable and enjoyable for you, and it needs to come from the heart.

> *Prayer needs to be comfortable*
> *and enjoyable for you, and it needs*
> *to come from the heart.*

God made us the way we are, so we need to approach Him without pretense and without thinking we have to sound a certain way in order for Him to hear us. As long as we are sincere, He will hear. Even if what is on our hearts cannot be articulated, He still hears and understands what it is. A heart lifted up to Him is precious in His sight, and He hears even words that cannot be uttered. Sometimes we hurt too bad to pray, and all we can do is sigh or groan—and God understands even that.

4. YOU DON'T HAVE TO BE PERFECT

James 5:16 declares that "the prayer of a righteous person is powerful and effective." Some people who struggle with prayer say, "Well, that's it. My prayers aren't working because I'm not righteous. Maybe if I start being more holy and doing everything right, my prayers will be more effective."

If we are born again, we are righteous. We may not *do* everything right, but we *are* 100 percent righteous through faith in Jesus all the time. Second Corinthians 5:21 tells us, "For He made Him who knew no sin to be sin for us, that we might become the righteousness of God in Him" (NKJV). There is a difference between righteousness and "right" behavior.

Righteousness describes our standing—our position or condition before God—*because of the blood of Jesus.* We cannot make ourselves righteous; only the blood of Jesus—His sacrifice on behalf of our sins—makes us righteous, as though we had never sinned at all. Based on the fact that Jesus paid the price for our sin when He suffered and died on the cross (1 Peter 2:24), God views us as righteous even though we still make mistakes. Because He sees us as righteous, we have a God-given right to pray and expect our prayers to be heard. God doesn't answer our prayers because we are good, but because He is good.

HOW TO HANDLE ANY SITUATION

I hope you have learned in this chapter that prayer truly is simple. James 5:13–14 says: "Is anyone among you in trouble? Let them pray. Is anyone happy? Let them sing songs of praise. Is anyone among you sick? Let them call the elders of the church to pray over them and anoint them with oil in the name of the Lord."

Based on these verses, how should people respond to problems? "Let them pray." This is a simple, three-word solution to the situations mentioned in James

5:13–14 and to anything else we may encounter in life. The Bible does not give us complicated instructions about what to do; it merely says, "Let them pray." So…

- When you don't know what to do, pray.
- When you have a need, pray.
- When you feel anxious or afraid, pray.
- When someone offends you or hurts your feelings, pray.
- When you are sick, pray.
- When you are discouraged or feel like giving up, pray.
- When someone you love is suffering, pray.
- When you have a problem of any kind, pray.

Whatever situation you find yourself in, pray before you do anything else. I know it's tempting to pick up the phone and tell a friend about a problem or to do an internet search to try to find the answers you need, but before doing anything else, take a minute and talk to God about what's going on in your life. Make prayer your first response to any circumstance, and it will be the easiest and most effective way to handle it. Your prayers can be short, uncomplicated, and not eloquent. And they can be imperfect. As long as you're sincere and filled with faith, God will hear.

Chapter 4

The Simplest Kind of Prayer

I don't think I can write about prayer without also writing about God's Word. It is such a treasure. It is filled with wisdom, direction, truth, and everything else we need in order to live purposeful, powerful, successful lives. When we incorporate the Word in our prayers, confessing it over every circumstance and situation, we bring the power of God's Word to bear on our lives and the things that are important to us. The word *confess* is defined as "to own; to acknowledge; to declare to be true, or to admit or assent to in words." This basically means "to say the same thing as," so when we confess God's Word, we are saying what He says and putting ourselves in agreement with Him. If we really want a deep and vibrant relationship with God, we need to agree with Him, and nothing will help us do that like praying and confessing the Word. The psalmist says to God in Psalm 119:49–50: "Remember your word to your servant, for you have given me hope. My comfort in my suffering is this: Your promise preserves my life."

Praying and confessing God's Word strengthens our knowledge of the Word and our faith in God, which increases the accuracy and effectiveness of our prayers.

Perhaps you have never heard the phrase *pray the Word* and are wondering how to do it. I think praying the Word, or "praying the Scriptures," as some people say, is the simplest form of prayer available to any believer. To pray the Word, we need to know the Word because we can only agree with God when we know what He has done and what He has said.

HOW TO PRAY THE WORD

The best way I know to help you learn to pray the Word if you haven't prayed this way before is to give you an example. Let's use Jeremiah 31:3, where God says through the prophet Jeremiah, "I have loved you with an everlasting love; I have drawn you with unfailing kindness."

If you are praying this scripture verse for yourself, you would say something like this: "God, Your Word says that You have loved me with an everlasting love and that You have drawn me with unfailing kindness. I thank You for loving me so much and for continuing to draw me closer to You with such kindness. Help me, Lord, to be conscious and aware of Your love for me."

If you were praying this same scripture for your friend Susie, who has been struggling to believe God really loves her, you would say something like, "God, Your Word says that You have loved Susie with an everlasting love and that You have drawn her with unfailing kindness. God, You know that Susie hasn't felt very secure in Your love lately, so I am asking You to override her emotions with the truth of this promise."

You can pray God's Word for yourself and for others. When you are in times of crisis or need, or when someone you know needs prayer, ask God to impress a Scripture verse upon your heart and help you pray it. As you do, I believe that your confidence in God's Word will grow, your faith will increase, and you will experience the awesome joy of answered prayer.

> *Ask God to impress a Scripture verse upon*
> *your heart and help you pray it.*

PRAYING THE WORD IN YOUR EVERYDAY LIFE

God's Word is designed to help us, direct us, and encourage us in our everyday lives, and we can find Bible verses or passages to pray in every situation. If you don't know what to pray, use a concordance (a book in which you find Scripture references based on key words) or do an internet search related to your situation. For instance, if you feel anxious and need peace, you could search for "scriptures on anxiety" or "scriptures about peace."

At times, we can find verses or passages that give us remarkably specific, detailed direction, and at other times we need to take a nugget of wisdom or a general spiritual principle and apply it to the matter with which we are dealing. For example, listed below are several common, specific circumstances and emotions and a few corresponding verses to pray for yourself or for someone else.

When you need to know God hears your prayers, you can pray:
- Psalm 6:9: "The Lord has heard my supplication; the Lord receives my prayer" (AMPC).
- Psalm 55:17: "Evening and morning and at noon I will pray, and cry aloud, and He shall hear my voice" (NKJV).

When you are afraid, you can pray:
- Isaiah 41:10: "So do not fear, for I am with you; do not be dismayed, for I am your God. I will strengthen you and help you; I will uphold you with my righteous right hand."
- Joshua 1:9: "Have I not commanded you? Be strong and courageous. Do not be afraid; do not be discouraged, for the Lord your God will be with you wherever you go."

When you are going through a season of difficulty or something that is wearing you out, you can pray:

- Isaiah 40:29: "He gives strength to the weary and increases the power of the weak."
- Isaiah 40:31: "But those who wait for the Lord [who expect, look for, and hope in Him] shall change and renew their strength and power; they shall lift their wings and mount up [close to God] as eagles [mount up to the sun]; they shall run and not be weary, they shall walk and not faint or become tired" (AMPC).
- Lamentations 3:22–23: "It is because of the Lord's mercy and loving-kindness that we are not consumed, because His [tender] compassions fail not. They are new every morning; great and abundant is Your stability and faithfulness" (AMPC).

If you find yourself saying things you shouldn't say, you can pray:

- Psalm 141:3: "Set a guard over my mouth, Lord; keep watch over the door of my lips."

- Psalm 19:14: "Let the words of my mouth and the meditation of my heart be acceptable in Your sight, O Lord, my strength and my Redeemer" (NKJV).

When you are stressed and under pressure, you can pray:

- Psalm 55:22: "Cast your cares on the Lord and he will sustain you; he will never let the righteous be shaken."
- Isaiah 26:3: "You will keep him in perfect peace, whose mind is stayed on You, because he trusts in You" (NKJV).

When you are struggling financially, you can pray:

- Psalm 34:9–10: "Oh, fear the Lord, you His saints! There is no want to those who fear Him. The young lions lack and suffer hunger; but those who seek the Lord shall not lack any good thing" (NKJV).
- Matthew 6:33: "But seek first the kingdom of God and His righteousness, and all these things shall be added to you" (NKJV).

- Philippians 4:19: "And my God will meet all your needs according to the riches of his glory in Christ Jesus."

When you are faced with a decision and don't know what to do, you can pray:

- Proverbs 3:5–6: "Lean on, trust in, and be confident in the Lord with all your heart and mind and do not rely on your own insight or understanding. In all your ways know, recognize, and acknowledge Him, and He will direct and make straight and plain your paths" (AMPC).
- Isaiah 42:16: "I will lead the blind by ways they have not known, along unfamiliar paths I will guide them; I will turn the darkness into light before them and make the rough places smooth. These are the things I will do; I will not forsake them."

When you are concerned or discouraged about the future, you can pray:

- Jeremiah 31:17: "There is hope for your future" (AMPC).

- Jeremiah 29:11: "For I know the thoughts and plans that I have for you, says the Lord, thoughts and plans for welfare and peace and not for evil, to give you hope in your final outcome" (AMPC).

**When you are not sure what God is doing
with you or what is going on in your life,
you can pray:**

- Psalm 37:23: "The steps of a [good] man are directed and established by the Lord when He delights in his way [and He busies Himself with his every step]" (AMPC).
- Isaiah 55:8–9: "'For my thoughts are not your thoughts, neither are your ways my ways,' declares the Lord. 'As the heavens are higher than the earth, so are my ways higher than your ways and my thoughts than your thoughts.'"

The examples above do not cover every single area of our lives, but hopefully you can see from them that God's Word does provide direction and ways we can pray in every situation we face.

Before we close this chapter, I want to encourage you to include thanksgiving often when you pray God's Word. When you need something from Him, and His Word says He has already done it, you can pray from a position of thanks instead of from a place of need. You'll read more about the power of thanksgiving in a later chapter, but for now let me simply say that putting your prayers in the context of gratitude will really make a difference: For example:

- Instead of praying to hear God's voice, thank Him that you do hear Him (John 10:27).
- Instead of praying to be set free, thank God for having already set you free (Galatians 5:1).
- Instead of asking God to have a good plan for your life, thank Him for already having a good plan (Jeremiah 29:11).
- Instead of praying that God will make you righteous, thank Him that He has already done so (2 Corinthians 5:21).
- Instead of praying for God to bless you, thank Him that you are already blessed with every blessing (Ephesians 1:3).

- Instead of praying for God to accept you, thank Him for already accepting you in Christ (Ephesians 1:6).

I encourage you to search the Scriptures and to memorize and meditate on as many as you possibly can. This way, God's Word will go deep into your heart, and you will have a well of wisdom and truth to draw from so you can include the Word as a vital part of your communication with God.

PART 2

How to Pray Powerful Prayers

Chapter 5

Practice the Habits of Powerful People Who Pray Powerfully

One of my prayers for you is that your prayers will be powerful, and that you will communicate with God in ways that bring His heart and His plans into your life and the lives of the people around you.

James 5:16 says: "The heartfelt and persistent prayer of a righteous man (believer) can accomplish much [when put into action and made effective by God—it is dynamic and can have tremendous power]" (AMP).

Prayers that "accomplish much" are powerful and effective. They make a difference. And any believer can pray powerful, effective prayers.

Your prayers can have an impact on your life, in the lives of people you love, on your neighborhood and your workplace, even in your nation and in the world.

> *Your prayers can have an impact*
> *on your life and in the lives*
> *of people you love.*

Maybe you know someone who, when you think about that person, causes you to say to yourself, "Wow! Her prayers are so powerful!" Or "When he prays, things change!" I have noticed that people who consistently pray powerful prayers understand the principles discussed earlier in this book. They know that prayer doesn't have to be long, complicated, or eloquent, and they understand that they don't have to be perfect. They may have some type of schedule or routine for their prayer times, but they aren't legalistic about it. They don't follow rules or formulas. They understand that simple, sincere, faith-filled prayers catch God's attention. *They pray powerful prayers because they have developed habits that are keys to effective prayer.* They live a life that incorporates the principles that cause prayer to make a difference.

There are many habits that contribute to powerful prayers, and there isn't space in this book to list or elaborate on them all. But over the next several chapters, let's explore some that I believe are most important. I hope you will make them part of your life and that, someday, people will look at you and say to themselves, "Wow! Her prayers are so powerful!" or "When he prays, things change!"

In this chapter, let's look at two habits that are vital to powerful prayer: praying according to God's will and staying focused in our prayers.

PRAY ACCORDING TO GOD'S WILL

The best way to pray effective prayers is to pray according to God's will—to sincerely want for ourselves what He desires for us. And the best way to make sure we are praying within God's will is to pray the Word as much as possible. As I explained in chapter 4, praying the Word means using a verse, a passage, or a principle in God's Word to back up what we are praying.

> *The best way to pray effective prayers is to pray according to God's will—to sincerely want for ourselves what He desires for us.*

Many places in the Bible let us know clearly what God's will is for all people because He specifies it. For instance, 2 Peter 3:9 says that He is "not wanting anyone to perish, but everyone to come to repentance." Therefore, we know we are praying within God's will when we pray for people to be saved.

Sometimes, when people think of praying the Word, the first thought that comes to mind is that the Bible doesn't give them the specific details they want—for example, whether or not to buy a new car. They will not find a passage that tells them to purchase a new car, but they will find scriptures that assure us that God cares for us and will meet our needs (1 Peter 5:7; Philippians 4:19). If a new car is a legitimate need, they can pray and believe that God's will is to meet that need. The Bible also teaches us to walk in wisdom (Proverbs 1:1–7; James 1:5), so we wouldn't want to buy a car if doing so would place a financial strain on us.

As another practical example of how God's Word leads us according to general principles, let's say someone is trying to decide whether to make a big purchase, something that costs a lot of money. It's something they really want, but it's not something they need in order to live (such as a house). Let's say that person is already in debt because, over the past few years, they've bought several other things they really wanted but didn't need. Scripture is full of advice on managing money. It also cautions people strongly against being in debt. So, the person will not read in the Bible "Don't buy that new boat" or "Don't buy tickets to the World Series this year." But the Bible does include a question from Jesus in Luke 14:28: "Suppose one of you wants to build a tower. Won't you first sit down and estimate the cost to see if you have enough money to complete it?" It also says in Romans 13:8, "Let no debt remain outstanding, except the continuing debt to love

one another, for whoever loves others has fulfilled
the law."

We often pray God's Word based on general
principles, and He then helps us apply them to our
specific situations. There are times, though, when
God's Word is remarkably specific. Let me give you
an example of how God's Word can help us in specific ways. I heard about a young woman who was
trying to decide whether to rent a house or buy
one. She was praying about this one day, and a certain Scripture reference came to her mind. It was
Acts 28:30. She wasn't familiar with the verse, but
she felt the Holy Spirit was leading her to look it
up. She was amazed when she read it: "For two
whole years Paul stayed there in his own rented
house and welcomed all who came to see him." Not
only did she decide to rent instead of buy, but she
asked for a two-year lease instead of the more typi-
cal one-year lease, and the landlord happily agreed
to it. She was blessed in that situation, and at the
end of two years, God led her to make other living arrangements. Let's believe God for miraculous
answers to our prayers.

*We often pray God's Word based on
general principles, and He then helps us
apply them to our specific situations.*

I'm sure you see what I mean when I say that the best way to pray effective prayers is to pray according to God's will, which we find in His Word. But sometimes, we want to pray for certain things, and we are not sure whether they are God's will for us. In those cases, we simply need to ask God to give them if it is His will to do so and to help us be satisfied with His decision. I don't want anything that is not God's will for me, because I know that having it would only make me unhappy.

There are times in life when, for various reasons, we don't pray according to God's will. Most often, this happens when our emotions are involved or when our human will (desire and power to choose) is strong. Sometimes we are so angry or so hurt that we pray prayers based on our emotions instead of on God's Word or His heart—and those prayers are not effective. When we pray something based on our human desires, thoughts, or emotions, we may be praying for something entirely different or far beneath what God wants for us. He always wants the best for us, and sometimes we would never pray for it because it hasn't entered our minds or because we are too upset to even consider it. We can be thankful that God doesn't answer prayers that are not according to His will.

> *Be thankful that God doesn't*
> *answer prayers that are not*
> *according to His will.*

I am sure that at times we all ask for things that may not be within God's will for us, but God knows our hearts, and He is gracious to us even when we ask for things that may not be best for us. I believe that if He cannot give us what we ask for, He will give us something better if we keep a good attitude and continue to pray for His will to be done in our lives.

When we pray in agreement with God's will, we will have what we ask for. We may have to wait because God's timing is part of His will, but it will come. We can say, "It's mine. I may not see it yet, but it's on its way."

Praying according to God's will may require patience, and it will definitely require faith. If you'll develop the habit of wanting and praying for God's will in all things, you'll see your prayers increase in power.

STAY FOCUSED

In addition to praying according to God's will, we also want to develop the habit of staying focused and being diligent to keep our hearts connected to heaven when we pray. This may sound simple, but it is foundational to powerful prayer. It's a necessary discipline if we want our prayers to make a difference.

Sometimes when we pray, we are distracted by the many pressures or activities of life, and before we know it, we find ourselves speaking words that have little meaning. We end up not concentrating on talking to God and not really paying attention to Him—and this is not a good way to have a prayer answered.

One of the best stories I know about focus is about taming lions. When a lion trainer goes into a cage with a lion, he takes three items: a whip, a stun gun, and a stool with three or four legs on it. He holds the stool with the legs pointing toward the lion. Why? Because a lion cannot focus on more than one thing at a time. When the lion sees more than one leg on the stool, it actually "freezes" and cannot move to attack the trainer.

In a way, when too much comes at us at one time, we can be like the lions and find ourselves unable to move. When we cannot focus, we are not effective or productive. Proverbs 4:25–27 says: "Let your eyes look straight ahead; fix your gaze directly before you. Give careful thought to the paths for your feet and be steadfast in all your ways. Do not turn to the right or the left; keep your foot from evil."

To pray effectively, we need to learn to stay focused not only in prayer but also in life. We need to know what God has called us to do, prioritize it, focus on it, pray about it, and watch as God answers our prayers and does great things through us.

> *To pray effectively, we need to learn
> to stay focused not only in prayer
> but also in life.*

Let me encourage you to know what God has called you to do and to pray consistently concerning those things. If you don't know what He has called you to do, don't be upset about it. Just ask God to help you stay focused on Him and His will for you each day. No one's prayers have as much effect on your life, family, and ministry as yours do. Prayer is like a laser beam. It is powerful, but it needs to be focused in an area until the desired results manifest. Whatever God assigns you to do, stay focused and remember that focused prayer is powerful prayer.

These first two habits—praying according to God's will and staying focused as you pray—will make a difference in your prayer life. If you'll incorporate just these two, I believe they'll make an impact on the way you pray and the results you see. But I want to mention several other habits. The next one is vitally important not only to prayer but to every area of your life. Let's take a look at that.

Chapter 6

Honor God

One of the most important aspects of our Christian lives—and a habit of powerful prayer—is honoring God through obedience to Him. Obedience reveals our love for God. Jesus says in John 14:15, "If you [really] love Me, you will keep and obey My commandments" (AMP). And 1 John 3:22 says: "We receive from Him whatever we ask, because we [watchfully] obey His orders" (AMPC). We simply will not make progress with God or excel in prayer unless we are willing to obey Him and grow in obedience.

> *Obedience reveals our love for God.*

Disobedience on any level is sin, and Isaiah 59:2 teaches us that sin separates us from God and causes

Him to not hear our prayers: "But your wrongdoings have caused a separation between you and your God, and your sins have hidden His face from you so that He does not hear" (NASB). This is especially true if we know we are sinning and continue to do so.

When I say *sin*, I am not talking about an innocent mistake or about something you do that you feel bad about—and for which you ask God's forgiveness. When we repent, God cleanses us and forgives us completely. In this context, I am talking about a pattern of intentional disobedience to God. We cannot knowingly, deliberately, and habitually sin and then expect God to give us a life filled with His blessings.

Does this mean we have to be perfect for God to answer our prayers? No. No one on earth is perfect, as I'm sure you have learned. Jesus is the only perfect One who ever lived. The rest of us are imperfect, and in His grace, God blesses us in our imperfections. He certainly knows we aren't perfect, but I think He also wants us to want to grow spiritually. Our attitudes need to send Him a message that says, "I don't want to stay this way. I want to grow spiritually. I want to change, and I'm pressing toward that mark. While

I'm on my way, I know I won't get everything right, but You are so gracious and merciful that I can still believe You will bless me while I keep maturing."

We hurt ourselves every time we do not obey God. For example, if God has told us to go and apologize to somebody, and we are too stubborn to say, "I'm sorry," we hurt ourselves and negatively affect our prayer lives.

Just as sin keeps us from praying effectively, obedience to God makes a way for our prayers to truly be effective and fruitful. When we obey Him, we position ourselves for answered prayers and great blessings. Just look at what the Bible says about the good things that come to those who obey.

- "Observe and obey all these words which I command you, that it may go well with you and your children after you forever, when you do what is good and right in the sight of the Lord your God" (Deuteronomy 12:28 NKJV).

- "The Lord your God will make you abound in all the work of your hand, in the fruit of your body, in the increase of your livestock, and in the produce of your land for good. For the Lord will again rejoice over you for good as He rejoiced over your fathers, if you obey the voice of the Lord your God, to keep His commandments and His statutes which are written in this Book of the Law, and if you turn to the Lord your God with all your heart and with all your soul" (Deuteronomy 30: 9–10 NKJV).

- "If they obey and serve Him, they shall spend their days in prosperity and their years in pleasantness and joy" (Job 36:11 AMPC).

- "If you keep My commandments, you will abide in My love, just as I have kept My Father's commandments and abide in His love" (John 15:10 NKJV).

Obeying God does bring blessings, including answered prayer, but it's not always easy. When I received my call into ministry in 1976, it was especially challenging for me to obey God. At the time, I was working a full-time job, trying to be a good wife, and raising three children. I barely had time for anything except survival, but I desperately needed to begin preparing for the teaching ministry God had put on my heart.

God began leading me to take a step of faith and quit my job so I could spend several hours each day praying and studying His Word. But I was afraid—even petrified—to quit my job. One reason for this was that I had little experience trusting God to meet my financial needs. He was calling me to a new level of faith, but because I was accustomed to taking care of myself, I found it difficult to be obedient.

In those days, our monthly bills exceeded my husband's income by forty dollars per month. If I quit my job, we would need to not only trust God for the forty dollars, but we would also have to rely on Him for money to cover extra expenses, such as car repairs, home maintenance, clothes, and other things we needed.

Because of our financial situation, I decided to quit my full-time job and get a part-time job. That was my way of partially obeying God and still having assurance that our needs would be met. In other words, I was not willing to trust Him fully.

After a few months, my new part-time job was

not going well. Normally, I was a very good employee, but I could not seem to do anything right at that job. Ultimately, I got fired, which is something that had never happened to me before. This incident taught me that God was serious when He led me to quit my job, start preparing for the teaching ministry, and trust Him to meet all our needs.

Over the next few years, I learned so much about God's goodness as I saw Him meet our needs in miraculous ways month after month. The things He did may not have appeared miraculous to someone else, but they were to me.

As we take steps of obedience to God, we learn to trust Him. We gain experience in trusting Him, and that increases our confidence. Let me caution you not to try to do what I did just because it worked for me. Be willing to do whatever God is asking *you* to do. Radical obedience will lead you into an exciting life with God, a life that will thrill and amaze you.

> *As we take steps of obedience to God,*
> *we learn to trust Him.*

I encourage you to make up your mind that you are going to be extremely, even radically, obedient to God. Obey Him in the big things and in the little things. A lifestyle of obedience to Him will bring blessings into your life that you have not even imagined yet, and it is a key to powerful, effective prayer.

REFUSE TO COMPROMISE

Honoring God through obedience is a habit we need to cultivate and grow in—not something we do sometimes and don't do at others. Even when we have a heart to honor and obey God, we can be tempted to compromise at certain times or in certain situations.

Just as God's Word teaches us to honor God through obedience, it also promises that He will hear our prayers if we seek to be consistently righteous in our walk with Him. Proverbs 15:29 says: "The Lord…hears the prayer of the [consistently] righteous (the upright, in right standing with Him)" (AMPC). What does it mean to be "consistently righteous"? Simply put, I think the best way to be consistently righteous is to refuse to compromise. It means not lowering the standards of obedience we find in God's Word or trying to find a way around them.

A person who compromises tends to go along with what everybody else wants to do, even though it may not be totally right. A compromiser knows when something is not right, but does it anyway, hoping to get away with it. We compromise when we know in our hearts—and even have the conviction of the Holy Spirit—that we should or should not do something. We often say, "I know I shouldn't do this, but…"

When our minds are filled with *I-shouldn't-buts*, we are saying, "God is showing me what to do, but I'm going to do what I want to." In these situations, we can only blame ourselves if we do not see the results we would like. But when we stand strong, do what the Holy Spirit is leading us to do, refuse to compromise, and devote ourselves to being consistently righteous, God hears our prayers. They accomplish much, and we can expect other blessings as well. His Word says:

- "The desire of the [uncompromisingly] righteous shall be granted" (Proverbs 10:24 AMPC).

- "The [uncompromisingly] righteous shall flourish like the palm tree [be long-lived, stately, upright, useful, and fruitful]" (Psalm 92:12 AMPC).
- "Light is sown for the [uncompromisingly] righteous...and joy for the upright in heart" (Psalm 97:11 AMPC).
- "The Lord loves the [uncompromisingly] righteous (those upright in heart and in right standing with Him)" (Psalm 146:8 AMPC).

Even though the Bible makes clear that those who are uncompromisingly righteous will be blessed, society seems to want us to compromise. If we refuse, they may call us religious fanatics or legalistic and rigid. Even some of our fellow Christians may accuse us of being legalistic when we try to live holy lives. I would rather go overboard trying to be holy than to go overboard taking an excess of liberties that will cause me to disobey God or miss a blessing. The world can easily pull us in its direction, but God is looking for those who push against the downhill moral slide the world seems to be in and live pure and holy lives without compromise.

> *God is looking for those who live pure*
> *and holy lives without compromise.*

If we are going to obey God (and remember, this is a key to effective prayer), we will have to overcome the opinions of people around us and dedicate ourselves to being consistently righteous. What does a consistently righteous person do? A consistently righteous person tries to do what is right all the time. They do it whether anyone is watching or not, knowing that God sees everything. They do it simply because it is the right thing to do.

Some people try to do what is right only when they are in trouble or when they need a miracle. For instance, someone might go to church only when they need a miracle, or they may behave better than they normally do only when they need help from God. It is amazing how "righteous" we can act when we need a breakthrough, but the consistently righteous person tries to honor God all the time. The consistently righteous person regularly does what is right because it honors God and reflects a heart of humility and a desire to obey Him. As you develop and grow in the habit of honoring God, your prayers will become increasingly powerful.

Chapter 7

Love

Of all the habits of people who pray powerful prayers, there is one that I believe we simply cannot do without. What is this all-important habit? Walking in love. Without love, our prayers will be like a noisy gong, clanging against the ceiling of heaven (1 Corinthians 13:1).

Jesus lets us know that love is His number one priority when He says, "I give you a new commandment: that you should love one another. Just as I have loved you, so you too should love one another" (John 13:34 AMPC). Loving people the way Jesus loves us may seem like a challenge to you. It may even seem impossible when you think about certain people in your life. But whenever God asks us to do something, He gives us the ability to do it. Love is a fruit of the Holy Spirit (Galatians 5:22–23), and the Holy Spirit lives and works in all believers.

He empowers us to do what God's Word teaches us to do.

The apostle Peter writes: "And *above all* things have fervent love for one another, for 'love will cover a multitude of sins'" (1 Peter 4:8 NKJV, italics mine). In other words, we are to have genuine, pure, fervent love for others above everything else we do. If we can only manage to do one thing in our lives, it should be to love other people.

The prerequisite for loving people is loving God and knowing that He loves us. In the context of loving Him, receiving His love, and extending His love to other people, we will find that our prayers are rich, vibrant, effective, and rewarding.

LOVE AND FAITH

Some people think great faith is the number one sign of spiritual maturity. But I believe walking in love is the true test of spiritual maturity, and I know it is essential to an effective prayer life. Our love walk energizes our faith walk. Galatians 5:6 says that what really counts is "faith activated and energized and expressed and working through love" (AMPC). We cannot pray effective prayers without having faith in

God, but love is what energizes our faith and makes it effective. When faith and love work together, our prayers will have tremendous results.

> *Our love walk energizes our faith walk.*

In the Old Testament, we read a lot about God's Law. The Law represents His requirements, meaning the way we are to live if we want to be blessed. We also read the writings of the prophets, which further help us understand what God desires. When the Pharisees asked Jesus what the greatest commandment in God's Law is (Matthew 22:36), Jesus said that all of God's Law and everything the prophets have written depends on one thing: "'Love the Lord your God with all your heart and with all your soul and with all your mind.' This is the first and greatest commandment. And the second is like it: 'Love your neighbor as yourself.' All the Law and the Prophets hang on these two commandments" (Matthew 22:37–40).

Jesus is basically saying in this passage that the bottom line in our walk with God is to love Him and

to love people. It's that simple. Walking in love is at
the heart of living a life of faith. Trying to walk in
faith without love is like having a flashlight without
a battery. We must be sure that we keep our love
battery charged at all times. Otherwise, our faith will
not work.

> *Walking in love is at the heart of living*
> *a life of faith.*

I believe Christians can run into problems when
we do not diligently pursue walking in love as a vital
part of our faith and relationship with God. We pray
to be blessed, we pray to be healed, we pray for our
children to make good choices, and we pray for the
things we want, but many people who pray do not
seem to desperately want to seek and pursue walking in love.

It is important to understand that love is not a
feeling; it is how we treat people. God tells us to
be good even to our enemies—to pray for and bless
them (Matthew 5:44). It is of great importance that
we have no unforgiveness in our heart because, if

we do, it will definitely hinder answered prayer. No matter what someone has done to us, we are never justified before God in holding unforgiveness against them. If we forgive, God will be our Vindicator.

I believe Satan is trying to build a stronghold of cold love in the hearts of believers. He wants us to have hard hearts that do not sense or care about the needs of other people. He wants us to be selfish and self-centered, thinking, *Somebody do something for me*, without reaching out to do anything for anybody else. He knows that faith works through love, and that without love, our faith amounts to nothing. We need to know that too and to be careful to develop a strong love walk as we seek to grow in faith and in other areas of our spiritual lives, including prayer. Love is the most important thing in the world.

WHAT LOVE IS

What does it mean to have the kind of faith that works through love? It means that we love people who we want to love and who are easy to love, and we also love those who are not so easy for us to love and may not seem to deserve to be loved. It means that when someone deserves for us to stay angry with them, we forgive—even if we believe our anger is justified. It means there will be times when we would love to talk about what someone did to us, but we choose to cover their offense instead because "love covers a multitude of sins" (1 Peter 4:8 AMPC).

Walking in love means we begin to have a heart like God, including being generous and giving with no strings attached, and being kind, merciful, forgiving, compassionate, helpful, and encouraging. In addition, it means wanting the best for people, believing the best about them, accepting them unconditionally, and never giving up on them.

Love is not talk or theory; it's action. First Corinthians 13 describes real love. It's often read at weddings, and it does apply to husbands and wives, but it also applies to everyone who seeks to walk in love in any kind of relationship—with siblings or extended family, with people at church, with friends and acquaintances, with coworkers, and with strangers we encounter as we go about our daily activities. We are to love people wherever we go and whatever we do—from running errands to checking out at a grocery store to working at our jobs to banking to attending sports events and to putting children to bed at night or waking them up in the morning.

> *Love is not talk or theory; it's action.*

First Corinthians 13:4 teaches us several qualities of love. It says that love is patient. A person who walks in love is not quick-tempered or easily angered. Instead of using the word *patient*, some Bible translations say in 1 Corinthians 13:4 that "love suffers long." In other words, it can put up with something and put up with it and put up with it and put up with it—it's hard to wear out real love! Love is also kind, which means that a person who walks in love is good to people; that person is considerate, gentle, and giving. Love doesn't envy or become jealous of other people for any reason. In fact, love rejoices when others succeed and when they get something they want—even if we want it too. Love isn't boastful or proud; it walks in humility before God and others.

According to 1 Corinthians 13:5, love isn't rude. Love says please and thank you and is careful not to hurt other people's feelings. Love always thinks of how things will make others feel. It does not just "seek its own" (NKJV); it prefers other people. Love is thoughtful. If someone is in a grocery store line with two full carts, and someone else is standing behind with two items, love backs up and lets the other person go first. Love is not easily angered, offended, or provoked, meaning that a person who walks in love is not touchy and gets over things quickly. That person does not hold grudges or seek revenge; love forgives and forgets. The person "thinks no evil" toward anyone (NKJV). Love always believes the best about people; it does not default to the negative, it is not suspicious, but believes the best of everyone.

In 1 Corinthians 13:6, we read that love "does not delight in evil but rejoices with the truth." This means love is happy when good triumphs in a situation and when truth is revealed. And in verse 7, we see that love "always protects, always trusts, always hopes, always perseveres."

Love sacrifices; love meets needs; love gives and gives and gives and gives and gives. In fact, real love does not have to be talked into giving; it is always looking for opportunities to express itself.

Love edifies. It does not tear down; it lifts up. Love encourages. Love listens.

Love is the law of the kingdom and the nature of God. Love is the demonstration and proof of our faith in God, and it is the secret to effective prayer.

> *Love is the demonstration of our faith in God and the secret to effective prayer.*

Before I go on, let me also mention that walking in love does *not* mean allowing someone to abuse you and use you. Loving someone does not mean that you have to be mistreated, but it does mean there will be times when you will stick with somebody you would rather get away from, as long as that person isn't doing anything illegal, immoral, or harmful. It means seeking and incorporating the heart of God for other people as you relate to them, and applying His wisdom in your relationships.

LOVE MAKES US USEFUL

We need to pray about our love walk, asking God to help us grow and mature in love and enable us to love people as He wants us to love them. I believe this is a prayer He loves to answer.

Notice something about 1 Corinthians 13. Before it describes what love is, it says in verse 2, "If I have the gift of prophecy and can fathom all mysteries and all knowledge, and if I have a faith that can move mountains, but do not have love, I am nothing." In the Amplified Bible, Classic Edition, the amplification of "nothing" is "a useless nobody."

If we want to be useful, we need to really think about this truth and start walking in love as the Bible encourages us:

- "Live a life worthy of the calling you have received…bearing with one another in love" (Ephesians 4:1–2).
- "What you heard from me, keep as the pattern of sound teaching, with faith and love in Christ Jesus" (2 Timothy 1:13).
- "And walk in love, as Christ also has loved us and given Himself for us" (Ephesians 5:2 NKJV).

LIVE THE GOLDEN RULE

Another biblical principle that will help us walk in love and reap great results when we obey it is found in Matthew 7:7–11:

> Ask and it will be given to you; seek and you will find; knock and the door will be opened to you. For everyone who asks receives; the one who seeks finds; and to the one who knocks, the door will be opened. Which of you, if your son asks for bread, will give him a stone? Or if he asks for a fish, will give him a snake? If you, then, though you are evil, know how to give good gifts to your children, how much more will your Father in heaven give good gifts to those who ask him!

Now let's look at the next verse: "So *in everything, do to others what you would have them do to you*, for this sums up the Law and the Prophets" (Matthew 7:12, italics mine). This verse is known as the Golden Rule.

I think many people approach Matthew 7:7–11

as one subject and Matthew 7:12 as an independent thought. We may think Matthew is suddenly going in a different direction, but he is basically saying: "If you ask and keep on asking, it will be given to you, but now here comes a condition: so then, if this is what you want to see happen—however you want other people to treat you, treat them that way first." This teaches us that loving others is a condition of powerful prayer. Remember, our faith won't work without love.

Treating others as we would like to be treated in every situation will bring peace and joy into our dealings with other people and lead to strong, fruitful relationships in which people do what God has called them to do and enjoy Him together.

I encourage you: whatever you want other people to do for you, do for them. If you want friends, be friendly. If you want gifts, give something away. If you want people to encourage you, encourage someone else. If you want people to pray for you, pray for others. You may think friendliness, gift giving, encouragement, and prayer are little things. But often it's the little things people do that make relationships great. At the same time, it's the little things people don't do that can ultimately destroy relationships. So, in all things, big or small, treat people the way you want to be treated. That's a never-fail way to walk in love.

Chapter 8

Forgive

If we want to pray prayers that are powerful, we must approach God with clean hearts. A sure way to be clean before Him is to make sure we have forgiven everyone who has hurt or offended us. Forgiveness is not easy, but it is a prerequisite for effective prayer. We often think the people who have hurt us don't deserve our forgiveness. In fact, they may not even be sorry for what they did, but we need peace, and forgiving others is a way to have it. We must also ask ourselves if we deserve the forgiveness that God gives us, and we know that we don't.

Jesus says in Mark 11:25–26: "And whenever you stand praying, if you have anything against anyone, forgive him and let it drop (leave it, let it go), in order that your Father Who is in heaven may also forgive you your [own] failings and shortcomings and let them drop" (AMPC).

Jesus spoke these words to His disciples. They knew His teachings on forgiveness, but Peter, in particular, must have still found it a challenge. He asked Jesus one day, "Lord, how many times shall I forgive my brother or sister who sins against me? Up to seven times?" (Matthew 18:21).

Some translations render Jesus' response as "seventy-seven times" (Matthew 18:22 NIV, ESV), and others render it "seventy times seven" (AMP, NLT). The easiest way to understand this is to know that the number seven represents completion or perfection, so all Jesus was really saying was "Keep on forgiving and keep on forgiving and keep on forgiving."

GOD GIVES US GRACE TO FORGIVE

Even though we know we must forgive, forgiving those who hurt us is not easy, because our emotions are involved, and oftentimes, they tend to be stirred up and tender when we have been wounded or offended. We don't need to wait until we feel like forgiving someone, or we might never do it.

In order to forgive, we must realize that forgiveness is not something we feel; it is a decision we make. Our feelings will eventually follow the decision to forgive, but it may take some time before they do.

> *We don't need to wait until we feel like forgiving someone, or we might never do it.*

When we have been hurt, we don't feel like opening our hearts again to the people who hurt us. We may even think doing so is impossible. We want to shut them out of our lives and avoid them if at all possible. These are natural, human reactions, but they do not reflect the way God wants us to think and act. God loves us unconditionally and forgives us every time we ask His forgiveness. He expects us to forgive others, just as He forgives us. Think about Ephesians 4:32: "Be kind and compassionate to one another, forgiving each other, just as in Christ God forgave you."

I remember a time when Dave really hurt my feelings, and I could not seem to open my mouth to talk to him, let alone be friendly. As usual, the Holy Spirit was prompting me to behave in a godly way, but I had no strength to do it. I went to my office at home, where I frequently pray, and told God, "I am not coming out of here until You give me the grace to go out and talk to Dave as if he had never hurt my feelings. I know he didn't hurt me on purpose, and I want to drop it and let it go."

I not only prayed, but I looked up several scriptures on forgiveness and the danger of staying angry. Before long, I felt my heart softening and opening up to Dave again. I was able to go out of the room and resume my normal relationship with him.

I encourage you to pray when you need to forgive. Don't just *try* to forgive, but depend on God to give you grace, which enables you to do the hard things in life. Too often we try without going to God for help. When we do that, we are basically operating on our own, but we need to remember what Philippians 4:13 says: "I can do all things through Christ who strengthens me" (NKJV).

Prayer makes a way for God to work, so when you need to forgive, pray until you are released from the anger you feel and are able to be obedient to God.

When we forgive, we are being Christlike; we are acting as God acts—because He is a forgiving God. Forgiveness is manifested mercy; it is love in action—not love based on a feeling, but love based on a decision, an intentional choice to obey God. In fact, I believe forgiveness is one of the highest forms of love. And, as we discussed in the previous chapter, I believe that love is a vital key to powerful and effective prayer. Forgiveness and love go hand in hand, and expressing them honors and glorifies God, puts us in agreement with Him, and causes us to obey His Word. This brings great power to our prayers.

UNFORGIVENESS HINDERS OUR PRAYERS

Not only do I believe that forgiving people is essential to powerful prayer, but I also believe that unforgiveness is probably the number one reason prayers are not answered. I would venture to say that Christians lose more ground spiritually and suffer more emotionally, mentally, and relationally because of what is given up in a believer's life through unforgiveness than for any other reason or through anything else.

God's Word includes many scriptures that emphasize the importance of forgiveness, which is nothing
more than treating others the way God treats us. I
do not think we can find any clearer biblical command to forgive than Ephesians 4:32, which makes
the instruction to forgive clear, saying that we are to
forgive "one another [readily and freely], as God in
Christ forgave you" (AMPC).

Because we live in a fallen world full of people
who are imperfect, including you and me, we cannot
avoid being hurt, offended, victimized, or betrayed.
We will have reasons to be upset and angry, but unre-
solved anger turns to bitterness and unforgiveness—
and that will hinder our prayers. In fact, Ephesians
4:26 says, "When angry, do not sin; do not ever let
your wrath (your exasperation, your fury or indigna-
tion) last until the sun goes down" (AMPC).

We simply cannot hold on to anger and har-
bor unforgiveness in our hearts if we want God to
answer our prayers. Yet all of us have reasons we
may not want to forgive certain people for certain
things. But if we walk in obedience to God and His
Word, we must forgive. In other words, whatever

we have against anyone must be forgiven. No matter how major or how minor an issue seems, we have to let it go. We do not wait until we feel like forgiving; we forgive by making an intentional choice, a willful decision to let a matter drop. The quicker we forgive, the easier it is to do. When we do, we make a way for our prayers to be answered.

> *If we walk in obedience to God*
> *and His Word, we must forgive.*

Chapter 9

Have a Humble, Grateful Heart

First Peter 5:5 says that "God resists the proud, but gives grace to the humble" (NKJV). When we pray and ask for God's grace in a situation, humility paves the way for it. Developing a habit of humble dependence on God and thankfulness for all He does for us brings power to our prayers. In this chapter, let's look first at humility and then at gratitude.

APPROACH GOD IN HUMILITY

Every time we pray, we should approach God with humility, reverence, and awe. When we are humble, we recognize our need for God and our need for other people. We also act graciously toward others and honor them, preferring them over ourselves.

Look at some of the observations God's Word makes about people who walk in humility:

- "He leads the humble in justice, and He teaches the humble His way" (Psalm 25:9 AMP).
- "For the Lord takes delight in his people; he crowns the humble with victory" (Psalm 149:4).
- "When pride comes, then comes disgrace, but with humility comes wisdom" (Proverbs 11:2).
- "The reward of humility and the reverent and worshipful fear of the Lord is riches and honor and life" (Proverbs 22:4 AMPC).
- "Humble yourselves before the Lord, and he will lift you up" (James 4:10).

You can see that humility is powerful, and it is an attitude that God blesses.

The opposite of humility is pride. When we are proud, we do not think we need God or anyone else. We feel self-sufficient, we are self-reliant, and we think we are better than other people. The Bible contains many warnings against pride, and one of the strongest is Proverbs 16:5, which says: "The Lord detests all the proud of heart. Be sure of this: They will not go unpunished."

Pride will keep our prayers from being answered, and we must deal with our pride if we want God to hear and respond to us when we pray. To overcome the sin of pride, we need to ask God to help us develop humility and do everything we can to cultivate humility in our hearts. We need to be humble not only before God but also in our relationships with other people.

One of the best ways to practice humility is through confession. James 5:16 says, "Confess to one another therefore your faults (your slips, your false steps, your offenses, your sins) and pray [also] for one another, that you may be healed and restored [to a spiritual tone of mind and heart]" (AMPC).

> *We must deal with our pride if we want God*
> *to hear and respond to us when we pray.*

If the power to be healed and restored can come through confession and prayer, then we need to know how to confess and how to pray.

Confessing our faults to someone and asking for prayer requires first that we find someone we truly trust, and second that we are willing to humbly share our struggles. If this is difficult for you, ask God to help you grow in humility, because the results are amazing if you find a friend you can trust and share with that person, "I'm struggling in this area, and I don't want to, but I'm hurting, and I need you to pray for me."

I remember feeling jealous of a friend who got something I had asked God for but had not received yet. I did not want to feel the way I felt, and I knew it was wrong, but I could not seem to break free from resenting her blessing and wishing it were mine. The jealousy was even causing me to be cold in my attitude toward her. As I read James 5:16 one day, I decided I needed to humble myself and ask someone to pray for me. I did not mind talking to God about my problem, but I didn't look forward to telling anyone else (that was pride!). I ended up telling my husband I was feeling jealous of my friend. I confessed it as sin and asked him to pray for me. Sharing my feelings was embarrassing for me, but it also set me free.

Based on this experience and many others, I can assure you that humbly seeking help when we need it can set us free from bondage to sin. When we are really struggling with something, if we will go humbly to a trusted person who knows how to pray—someone who will not judge us or broadcast our concerns to others—and simply share our challenges and ask for prayer, the results can be tremendous.

There is no need to be ashamed to tell a true, prayerful confidant what our difficulties are. This is one way we exercise humility. Satan likes to keep things hidden. He is pleased when we try to handle situations ourselves, even when we know we cannot, because that is pride. When we ask others to help us, we are being humble. Humility pleases God, and He releases power to help us overcome.

We all need help. We all struggle, and your challenges probably are no worse than anyone else's. God has designed His family to need one another. Sometimes we simply cannot carry the loads of our lives alone, and sometimes we are too stubborn or too proud to ask for the help we need. Remember, God resists the proud; therefore, we know that pride is a hindrance to answered prayer. But He sends

His grace to the humble, and He hears and answers prayers prayed from humble hearts.

LIVE WITH GRATITUDE

I believe humility and gratitude go hand in hand. Humble people are grateful people. God does so much for us—much more, I believe, than we know. When we genuinely appreciate His goodness and have thankful hearts for all He has done, He is inclined to continue to bless us.

> *Humility and gratitude go hand in hand.*

The Bible is full of scriptures that instruct us to be thankful, and it specifically teaches us to be thankful when we pray. For example, Philippians 4:6 says, "Do not be anxious about anything, but in every situation, by prayer and petition, with thanksgiving, present your requests to God." And 1 Thessalonians 5:16–18 says, "Rejoice always, pray continually, give thanks in all circumstances; for this is God's will for you in Christ Jesus."

We can *be* thankful even if we don't *feel* thankful.

When we pray, there is always something we can thank God for. It may be a beautiful day or good health or a meal or a job that pays the bills or a friend or clean water or heat or air-conditioning. Even if we feel disappointed in some way, we also have many reasons to be thankful, and we should focus on those. Thanksgiving keeps us focused on God and appreciating the blessings we do have, not on ourselves and what we still want but don't have. I heard someone say, "What if you woke up today and all you had was what you were thankful for yesterday?" If that were the case, I am sure our thankfulness would increase dramatically.

The apostle Paul certainly endured his share of difficulty. He was beaten, stoned, and shipwrecked, often in danger, and hungry and thirsty at times (2 Corinthians 11:25–27). Even though he knew much suffering during his life and had reason to complain about some of his circumstances, he still said, "I know what it is to be in need, and I know what it is to have plenty. I have learned the secret of being content in any and every situation, whether well fed or hungry, whether living in plenty or in want" (Philippians 4:12).

I believe thankfulness is part of contentment. Based on Paul's other writings, I believe he was not only content but also thankful, no matter what his situation. Remember, 1 Thessalonians 5:18 says, "Give thanks in all circumstances," and Paul wrote these words.

We need to stay thankful in every situation, no matter how we feel. True gratitude is not only being thankful when things are going well but also remaining steadfast when dealing with life's struggles, obstacles, and disappointments. When we can be thankful regardless of our circumstances, we can pray powerful, effective prayers.

People who are humble and thankful are powerful in prayer. When we are humble, we can count on His grace to be there for us when we need it. And when we are thankful, I believe God is happy to do more for us than He has ever done before.

> *People who are humble and thankful*
> *are powerful in prayer.*

Chapter 10

Focus on Others

Many times, when we pray, we think first about our own needs and desires. But focusing on other people as we pray—called "intercession" because we intercede for them, asking God to help or bless them—is an important aspect of powerful prayer. The apostle Paul instructed the Ephesians: "Pray in the Spirit on all occasions with all kinds of prayers and requests. With this in mind, be alert and *always keep on praying for all the Lord's people*" (Ephesians 6:18, italics mine).

We can pray for ourselves, and we can pray for radical blessings for ourselves, but we need to also be aware of others and include them and their needs in our prayers.

I frequently hear of four or five people who need prayer, and just when some of those prayers are answered, I become aware of other people to pray for. This may happen in your life too. You hear of someone who recently lost a loved one, someone who needs a job, someone who needs a place to live, someone who just received a bad report from the doctor, someone whose child is sick, or someone whose spouse just left them. People have all kinds of needs, and they need our prayers.

ASK THE HOLY SPIRIT TO LEAD YOU AS YOU PRAY

God wants us to pray for one another with loving, selfless attitudes, because our prayers cannot be answered otherwise. I want to challenge you to ask God to give you someone to pray for. It may be someone you know well or someone you have never met. You may not even know what to pray for in this person's life, but sometimes, if you just get quiet in His presence and ask, He will begin to show you things and help you pray. I personally know this type of intercessory prayer to be extremely valuable, rewarding, and effective. I certainly appreciate it when people pray for me, and I am sure you do too. God places a priority on people. Each person is infinitely valuable to Him, and if we follow His example, people will become our priority also.

Notice what the apostle Paul writes to the believers in Colossae. He says he has not stopped praying for them since he first heard of them. Notice also *how* he prays for them, focusing on their spiritual needs and their spiritual growth:

> For this reason, since the day we heard about you, we have not stopped praying for you. We continually ask God to fill you with the knowledge of his will through all the wisdom and understanding that the Spirit gives, so that you may live a life worthy of the Lord and please him in every way: bearing fruit in every good work, growing in the knowledge of God.
>
> Colossians 1:9–10

If you don't know how to pray for someone, this prayer would be an excellent model. You can pray for others to be filled with the knowledge of God's will, to "live a life worthy of the Lord and please him in every way," to bear fruit in every good work, and to grow in the knowledge of God. I can't imagine that anyone wouldn't appreciate this kind of prayer. In addition, ask the Holy Spirit to lead you as you pray. If He puts something on your heart for someone, simply pray about it.

TREAT EVERYONE WELL, ESPECIALLY THOSE IN NEED

In addition to focusing on others when we pray, it is also important to God that we treat people well. He loves everyone and doesn't want anyone to be treated badly. If you have ever been mistreated, then you know how painful it is. If you want to pray powerful prayers, be sure to be good to people.

Treating all people well certainly includes expressing kindness and generosity to our inner circle of family and friends. It also includes having nice manners and being good to those who help us or work for us (which includes paying people well). And treating people well also extends to our communities and to the world, especially to those who are in need.

I believe that many of our prayers go unanswered at times because we do not treat others well, and we do not extend mercy or compassion to people in difficult situations. Proverbs 21:13 says: "Whoever stops his ears at the cry of the poor will cry out himself and not be heard" (AMPC). This means that when I do not pay attention to people in need and do not do anything to help them, God may not be inclined to answer my call for help when I have a need.

First John 3:17–18 (AMPC) says,

> But if anyone has this world's goods (resources for sustaining life) and sees his brother and fellow believer in need, yet closes his heart of compassion against him, how can the love of God live and remain in him? Little children, let us not love [merely] in theory or in speech but in deed and in truth (in practice and in sincerity).

We may close our hearts of compassion when we hear about people who are needy for several reasons. First, we may think someone should help them, but it doesn't occur to us that we are the "someone" who should do it. I believe that God's people are called to care for the poor and needy.

The second reason we may close our hearts to

someone in need is that we may be afraid that person will take advantage of us. All I can say to this is that we should refuse to be taken advantage of. We need to be led by the Holy Spirit, do what we know is right, and serve others well without allowing ourselves to be exploited.

The third reason I want to mention is that some people feel overwhelmed by the depth or the volume of the needs they see. People may actually become hardened to them simply because they hear of so many needs. These days, news reports are filled with tragedy and disasters on a daily basis, and we should allow each one to touch our heart.

James 1:27 reveals the secret to having pure religion before God, which is "to look after orphans and widows in their distress." God's heart for orphans and widows can be seen throughout the Bible, but I believe the phrase "orphans and widows" describes anyone who is hurting, lonely, oppressed, or in need of anything, and we can help alleviate their loneliness with kind words and helpful deeds. When we do not extend the love of God to people in these situations, prayers will be hindered. As followers of Christ, we need to be a blessing to people but especially to the poor and needy and to the orphans and widows. As we do, we will be obeying His Word and expressing the love of God to others.

Consider Isaiah 58:6–9, which speaks of the kind of fasting God has chosen. First, it mentions bringing freedom to the oppressed (v. 6). Then it says: "Is it not to share your food with the hungry and to provide the poor wanderer with shelter—when you see the naked, to clothe them, and not to turn away from your own flesh and blood?" (v. 7). As a result, here's what we can expect:

Then your light will break forth like the dawn, and your healing will quickly appear; then your righteousness will go before you, and the glory of the Lord will be your rear guard. Then you will call, and the Lord will answer; you will cry for help, and he will say: Here am I.

Isaiah 58:8–9

In this passage, all God is really encouraging us to do through the prophet Isaiah is to be good to people. The result? God Himself will hear our prayers and say, "Here I am. What do you need? What can I do for you?"

Chapter 11

Live with Unwavering Expectation

One of the keys to powerful prayer is asking God for what we need *and continuing to pray* until we see His power working on our behalf or in our situation. Prayer is not something we do once or a few times, and then walk away. We need to build the habit of perseverance and expecting God to answer us, no matter how long it takes or how many obstacles we may face. This attitude of persistence and expectation is critical to effective prayer. Let's look at these two qualities and focus first on perseverance.

PERSEVERING PRAYER IS POWERFUL

Think again about James 5:16, and notice that it says, "The heartfelt and *persistent* prayer of a righteous man (believer) can accomplish much" (AMP; italics mine). The kind of prayer that accomplishes much is heartfelt and persistent, meaning that it doesn't quit. Even when an answer to prayer seems delayed, we are to continue to pray and not stop just because we have been praying a long time and are starting to wonder if God will answer. When the Holy Spirit leads us to pray, we are to persevere.

> *When the Holy Spirit leads us to pray,*
> *we are to persevere.*

Soon after Jesus taught His disciples to pray, He encouraged them to persevere in prayer, saying:

Ask and keep on asking and it shall be given you; seek and keep on seeking and you shall find; knock and keep on knocking and the door shall be opened to you. For everyone who asks and keeps on asking receives; and he who seeks and keeps on seeking finds; and to him who knocks and keeps on knocking, the door shall be opened.

Luke 11:9–10 AMPC

These verses teach us that Jesus wants us to persevere in prayer; He wants us to ask boldly and tenaciously. To be bold in prayer doesn't mean to ask disrespectfully or have a demanding attitude. It means we ask reverently but confidently. When we pray and keep on praying, our prayers will be effective, and we will receive the answers we need—in God's way and on His schedule.

Jesus once told a parable about a persistent widow who continued to ask an unjust judge to give her justice and legal protection from her adversary (Luke 18:3). For quite some time, he refused her request. But he finally said to himself, "Because this widow continues to bother me, I will give her justice and legal protection; otherwise by continually coming she [will be an intolerable annoyance and she] will wear me out" (Luke 18:4–5 AMP). She didn't give up, and the judge did what she asked him to do. If perseverance gets the attention of an unjust judge, how much more will our just God move in our behalf when we persevere?

The reason Jesus told this story, according to Luke 18:1, was to emphasize that we should always "pray and not give up and lose heart" (AMP). He told this parable to His disciples as a way of teaching them, and us, to persevere in prayer.

A blind man named Bartimaeus was also persistent in his asking Jesus for what he needed, shouting continually, "Jesus, Son of David, have pity and mercy on me [now]!" (Mark 10:47 AMPC).

I can just imagine people saying, "Man, shut up! Leave Him alone! You're making a ruckus here. You're making a scene. Be quiet!" But the Bible says that when people told this blind man to "keep still," he "kept on shouting out all the more" (Mark 10:48 AMPC). He knew that Jesus was his only hope, so he refused to quit crying out to Him. As a result, Jesus stopped what He was doing and healed Bartimaeus right there on the spot (Mark 10:51–52).

> *Do not give up on prayer.*

One main reason people do not experience victory in prayer (as well as in other areas) is simply that they give up too soon. They get discouraged, often because they don't see quick answers, and they don't persevere. I urge you not to give up on prayer. Keep praying, no matter what happens. When we quit praying, we play into the enemy's hand. He is the one who tempts us to say things like:

- "I'll never be blessed."
- "I guess I wasn't called into ministry after all."
- "Well, I guess I'll never have a better job."
- "I'll never graduate from college."
- "I guess I'll never be able to move to a better place."
- "I'll never get married."
- "I'll always be in debt."
- "I'll never lose weight."
- "I'll always be the one who gets left out."

Attitudes like these are likely to guarantee that we will not receive anything. Thoughts and words such as these often become self-fulfilling prophecies. Instead of thinking and talking about the *I'll nevers*, we need to be thinking, speaking, and praying according to God's Word, confessing what He says about us, not what we think or feel. For example:

I know who I am in Christ. I intend to be an overcomer, God, because Your Word says that I can be. I am more than a conqueror through Christ, who loves me [Romans 8:37]. Greater is He who is in me than he who is in the world [1 John 4:4]. I can do all things through Christ who strengthens me [Philippians 4:13]. You meet all of my needs [Philippians 4:19]. I am going to have everything You want for me. I'm coming out of this pit of negativity I've been in lately, and I'm going to do great things, with Your help. In Jesus' name.

This type of prayer and confession agrees with God's Word and, prayed persistently, will be powerful and yield great results. In fact, any type of prayer the Holy Spirit inspires us to pray and gives us grace to keep praying will be effective if we simply don't give up on it. Simply thanking God that your answer is on the way is a type of persistent prayer. When I think of a prayer I have prayed and not received an answer to, I often just thank God that He is working. This is a way of saying to Him, "I trust that You are working on this situation, and at just the right time the breakthrough will come."

Keep letting God know that you believe His promises and trust Him to be faithful. This leads us to think about expecting God to answer us when we pray.

> *Let God know that you believe His promises*
> *and trust Him to be faithful.*

EXPECT GOD TO ANSWER YOU

There was a time in my prayer life when I felt I would burst with expectation. Every time I prayed, I prayed with tremendous faith, fully expecting God to do exactly as I had requested. Then, for some reason, I lost that "edge" to my prayer life, and my sense of expectation began to fade. But God did not let me stay that way for long. He began dealing with me, encouraging me to be aggressive again in my expectations and to express them as I prayed with confidence that He would do great things in the world and in my life. I am not talking about being presumptuous, but about praying prayers filled with God-given expectation, God-given desires, and God-given vision—prayers that are prayed in true faith from a pure heart.

As I returned to a high level of expectation, I prayed like this: "God, in Jesus' name, I am expecting favor everywhere I go today. I am expecting favor from You and favor with everyone with whom I come in contact." I prayed prayers such as "God, I am expecting good news today. I am expecting to be amazed at the great things You do." When I prayed this way, it was amazing how many times the phone rang and someone said something incredibly encouraging. Sometimes, people even said, "Joyce, I've got good news for you." God wants us to be filled with positive expectation, because that's what hope is.

> *God wants us to be filled with positive expectation, because that's what hope is.*

Many people do not pray for good news because they fear being disappointed. That's not a godly attitude. If we want to pray effective prayers and see God's power released in our lives, we need to have attitudes that are pleasing to Him. We need to have positive expectations instead of negative ones. Our basic approach to life needs to align with faith and hope and good expectations, because the Bible says that without faith it is impossible to please God (Hebrews 11:6) and that hope will never disappoint us (Romans 5:5). There is nothing negative about God; there is nothing in Him or in His actions that will ever disappoint us; everything He does is for our good—so that's what we need to expect as we pray. We should not pray and then *wonder* if God will do anything at all; we should pray *expecting* God to do even more than we have asked.

> *We should pray* expecting *God to do even more than we have asked.*

I encourage you to approach God with confident expectation when you pray. Ask for and expect big things from Him. Ephesians 3:20 says God "is able to do exceedingly abundantly above all that we ask or think, according to the power that works in us" (NKJV). Look also at this verse from the Amplified Bible, Classic Edition. It says that God "is able to [carry out His purpose and] do superabundantly, far over and above all that we [dare] ask or think [infinitely beyond our highest prayers, desires, thoughts, hopes, or dreams]." Did you catch that? God can do "superabundantly, far over and above all" that we would ever dare to ask or even *think* to ask and *infinitely beyond* our "highest prayers, desires, thoughts, hopes, or dreams." This is amazing—and it should give us all the confidence we need to pray with high expectations. Personally, I would rather pray big prayers with bold faith and great expectations and receive half of what I prayed for than pray little prayers with no faith and get it all.

Notice that Ephesians 3:20 says God does "exceedingly abundantly above all that we ask or think, *according to the power that works in us*" (NKJV, italics mine). That is another important phrase in Ephesians 3:20, and we need to pay attention to it. The Amplified Bible, Classic Edition says that

God can do so much more than we can even ask or imagine "by (in consequence of) the [action of His] power that is at work within us." What is the power that works in us? It is the power of God. It works in us through His Holy Spirit, who lives in us, and it works through simple, believing prayer.

When we realize that the power of God is at work in us, we are able to pray expectantly. At the same time, expectancy carries its own kind of power—the power of hope, the power of faith. God's power is released when we pray in faith, trusting and believing Him, because faith pleases Him. Expectancy is an attribute of faith. Faith reaches into the spiritual realm and expects God's supernatural power to show up and do what no person on earth could do. Doubt, on the other hand, is afraid nothing good will happen. The person who prays halfhearted prayers and then doubts that those prayers will be answered has no confidence or expectation. This is a negative attitude that does not please God. He blesses faith, but He doesn't tend to bless doubt. We are powerless when we live with doubt, disappointment, and a lack of confidence in God.

> *When we realize that the power of God is at work in us, we are able to pray expectantly.*

Think about a time when you were not sure God would come through for you. You were not able to pray truly powerful prayers, were you? Now remember a time when your heart trusted completely in God, and you *knew* He would come through for you. You were able to pray persistently then—with a certain sense of power and with confidence—weren't you? This is the power of expectation in prayer. Even if things don't work out exactly the way you hoped they would, trust God to know what is best for you, persevere in prayer, and keep expecting Him to do great things.

Chapter 12

Break through the Barriers to Effective Prayer, Part 1

Now that you have learned some of the habits of powerful prayer, let's think about some of the barriers to effective prayer. We need to know not only what to do, as the habits of powerful prayer teach us, but we also need to know what *not* to do when we pray. If we are going to invest our time and energy in prayer, we want to do everything within our power to get good results and break through the things that will keep our prayers from being powerful.

The eight barriers to effective prayer that we will focus on in this chapter and the next one are:

1. Prayerlessness
2. Sin
3. Wrong motives

4. Doubt and unbelief
5. Worry
6. Negative speech
7. Lack of boldness
8. Not relating properly to authority

Let's get started by looking at the first barrier, which seems obvious, but it is one I do want to address: prayerlessness.

1. PRAYERLESSNESS

To say that prayerlessness is a barrier to effective prayer does seem obvious. But sometimes people struggle with unanswered prayers without realizing they haven't really prayed. Maybe they thought about the situation, intended to pray later, mentioned it to their church friends, or hoped it would change, but they haven't specifically prayed. I know this may seem overly simplistic, but it's true: Our prayers are not answered when we do not pray. James 4:2 says, "You do not have because you do not ask God." We have to ask for what we want and need. Sometimes we work on situations in our minds, or talk about them with our friends, or wish or hope, but we do not pray. Thinking, wishing, hoping, and talking with others are not prayer; only *prayer* is prayer. Prayer is going to the Father in Jesus' name and asking Him for what we need. When we have a need or a situation that concerns us, we are only praying when we talk to God about it.

> *Our prayers are not answered when we do not pray.*

Did you know that God is waiting for us to make requests of Him in prayer? Consider Matthew 7:7: "Ask and it will be given to you; seek and you will find; knock and the door will be opened to you." This verse teaches us that God is ready to act for us, according to His perfect timing, if we will only pray.

I once had an employee who often complained about how much work he had to do. I don't think he even realized he was complaining, but it annoyed me. He was irritating me. I fussed and fumed over it in my heart, got aggravated, thought negative thoughts, and actually began to complain about my employee who was complaining! Then one day I

realized I had never actually prayed about his negative attitude. So, I simply asked God to cause him
to stop complaining about his workload and to be
thankful and positive.

The very next day, when I saw the man, he made
a positive comment about his job—the first one I
had heard in a long time. He mentioned that he had
some time to rest and things were getting better.
Wow! God was ready to help me, but He was waiting until I prayed.

My prayerlessness was just as wrong as my
employee's complaining. I actually contributed to the
problem and was hindering God by being too pas-
sive to open a door for Him to work through prayer.
I thought about the problem, resented the problem,
talked about the problem, and got aggravated about
the problem, but literally months went by before I
prayed. As soon as I did, God intervened.

Learn from my mistake, and don't let a negative
situation continue in your life or in the lives of your
loved ones because you fail to pray about it. Prayerlessness hinders God from working in your life and
the lives of your loved ones.

2. SIN

We need to understand not only how the positive elements of an issue increase effectiveness in prayer, but also how its negative aspects cause problems in our prayer lives. This book includes an entire chapter on honoring God through obedience, which is a good, positive habit. In that chapter, I mentioned that sin is a hindrance to powerful prayer, which is certainly a negative, and I want to elaborate a bit more on that point because it is so important.

Psalm 66:18 says, "If I regard iniquity in my heart, the Lord will not hear me" (AMPC). *Iniquity* is another word for *sin*. So this verse teaches us that sin we are aware of and refuse to deal with is a barrier to effective prayer. None of us is perfect. We may all have something in our lives that displeases God, but it may be unintentional, and we may not even realize it. But once God convicts us of sin and makes us aware of it, we must deal with it. Otherwise, we are regarding iniquity in our hearts, and in that case, God will not hear us.

If we have sin hidden in our hearts, we cannot pray with confidence that our prayers will be effective and that God will answer them. We must be willing to confess it, repent, and receive God's forgiveness. We also need to do whatever the Holy Spirit leads us to do in addition to confession and repentance, such as working with Him to change our behavior, apologizing to someone we hurt, or making restitution in some way. Dealing with sin in these ways helps if we want to keep the lines of communication open with God. God knows our sins anyway, so there is no point in trying to hide them. Sometimes we ignore our sin until we forget about it, or we may not realize we have sinned. In these cases, it is good to do as David did and ask God to reveal our "hidden (unconscious, unintended) faults" and sins (Psalm 19:12 AMP).

For example, if the Holy Spirit brings to mind a situation in which we did not tell the truth, we cannot think, *Oh, that's no big deal. It was just an innocent little white lie.* We cannot take something He shows us and sweep it under the rug or decide it does not really matter. Instead, we have to admit that we have sinned, repent for lying, and receive His forgiveness.

Seemingly more often than not, what we call "little things" in our lives end up causing us major trouble because we allow them to grow into sinful habits and patterns. When God reveals sin in our lives, we need to stop what we are doing and repent. We need to revere Him so much that we take Him seriously. This means we do everything within our power to make sure that our relationship with Him is clean and pure and unobstructed by sin. Otherwise, our prayers will go unheard and unanswered.

3. WRONG MOTIVES

You know that James 4:2 says, "You do not have because you do not ask God," but I want you to also see James 4:3: "When you ask, you do not receive, because you ask with wrong motives, that you may spend what you get on your pleasures."

A motive is the "why" behind the "what." It is why we do what we do. In prayer, the reason we pray is much more important than the words we say. God looks at our hearts, and when He sees an impure motive, He doesn't answer prayer.

> *When God sees an impure motive,*
> *He doesn't answer prayer.*

Having a pure heart that truly loves God and loves people is always an acceptable motive to the Lord. Selfishness is unacceptable, revenge is unacceptable, manipulation and control are unacceptable, jealousy is unacceptable, and pride is unacceptable. In fact, anything that is selfish and unloving is an unacceptable motive.

I will admit that there was a time when I prayed diligently for God to help my ministry grow because I thought having a large, influential ministry would make me feel important. But do you know what happened? The ministry did not grow at all! In fact, it did not even *begin* to grow until my motives had been purified, the selfishness had been eliminated, and I could truthfully say that I only wanted the ministry to grow so that I could help more people.

Similarly, we may want to get our way in a situation and ask God to change someone's heart so they will be in agreement with us without even considering what might be best for the other person. God won't answer those types of selfish prayers. We may ask God to lead someone to apologize to us when, in reality, He wants us to apologize to them. Whatever happened may not have been our fault, but God still wants us to humble ourselves and be the ones to make peace. Why would He do something like this? Because humility is more valuable to us in the long run than having our feelings soothed because someone apologizes to us.

We need to honestly examine our motives, and we need to ask God on a regular basis to purify our hearts so that we can pray with the right motives. Many things changed in my life when I began to ask myself why I was doing what I was doing. Likewise, many of my prayers changed when I became more sensitive to the motives behind them. Taking a look at our motives can be painful, but it must be done if we truly desire to live before God with pure hearts and pray effective prayers.

4. DOUBT AND UNBELIEF

I think it goes without saying that faith is a major foundational key to powerful prayer. It is a powerful spiritual dynamic, and it is something God responds to and blesses. Without faith, Hebrews 11:6 says, "it is impossible to please God, because anyone who comes to him must believe that he exists and that he rewards those who earnestly seek him."

The opposite of faith is doubt or outright unbelief, and these are barriers to effective prayer. If we pray and then doubt, or pray and don't believe God is listening to us or that He cares about us, we erect a barrier between our prayer and God's answer.

We need to understand that faith is not without opposition. Satan attacks our minds with doubt, unbelief, and questioning, and when he does, we need to remember what we believe in our hearts, based on God's Word. We can believe something in our hearts even when our minds question it, and we need to go with what is in our hearts. We are not supposed to believe our doubts; we are supposed to doubt our doubts and believe our God.

> *We are supposed to doubt our doubts*
> *and believe our God.*

James 1:6–8 teaches us that when we doubt, we become double-minded and unstable, "like a wave of the sea, blown and tossed by the wind." Verse 7 says a person who doubts "should not expect to receive anything from the Lord." Once we have decided to follow God, we need to be solid in our faith and commitment to Him, refusing to change our mind when circumstances tempt us to question or doubt Him.

One of the keys to overcoming doubt and unbelief is found in Hebrews 12:2: "Looking away [from all that will distract] to Jesus, Who is the Leader and the Source of our faith...and is also its Finisher" (AMPC). Many times, doubt and unbelief start with distraction. When we are distracted—perhaps by problems or by the stresses of life—from God's promises or God's ability to come through for us, then we begin to doubt. We start thinking more and more about our circumstances or challenges, and then our faith begins to waver. But we need to do what Hebrews 12:2 says to do and keep looking to Jesus. In order to resist doubt and stay in faith, we need to stay focused on Him, on His goodness, on His ability to help us, on His love for us. And we need to merely glance at our problems. It isn't wise to live in denial of our problems, but we should refuse to pay too much attention to them.

Keeping our eyes off everything that would steal our faith or distract us from what God says is the key to standing firm in faith and the antidote to doubt and unbelief. God is the Source of our faith, and He finishes what He starts—so we have no reason to doubt Him. Remember, James 1:7 says we should not expect anything from God if we doubt. But as we stand in faith, believing Him, we can expect our prayers to be answered.

Chapter 13

Break through the Barriers to Effective Prayer, Part 2

Let's continue looking at the barriers to effective prayer, knowing that as we understand them, we grow in our ability to break through them. The more effectively we break through them, the more powerful our prayers will be.

5. WORRY

Another barrier to effective prayer is that after people pray, they worry. I mentioned Philippians 4:6 earlier, in the context of thanksgiving, but let's think about it now in the context of anxiety: "*Do not be anxious or worried about anything,* but in everything [every circumstance and situation] by prayer and petition with thanksgiving, continue to make your [specific] requests known to God" (AMP, italics mine).

Anxiety, which is another word for *worry*, means spending today trying to figure out tomorrow or spending today fearing tomorrow. Worry is meditating on our problems, but we are told to meditate on God's Word, not our problems, and we are privileged not to have anxiety about anything. We are blessed to be invited to trust God.

> *We are blessed to be invited to trust God.*

When we pray and then worry, we are focusing on our problems, not on God's power. We are not exercising trust in God. We are not fully releasing our burdens or needs to Him; we are "taking them back" and working them over in our minds. When we stay involved and insist upon keeping our hands on the situations we pray about, trying to change them or control them, we have not released them to God completely. We've asked Him to intervene, but we've gotten in His way instead of giving Him time to work. Sometimes, He does not have much freedom to answer our prayers. We say we trust God, but we want to have a backup plan just in case He does not come through for us.

The opposite of worry and anxiety is peace, and if we are going to live in peace, we need to learn how to live our lives one day at a time. Jesus says in Matthew 6:34, "So do not worry or be anxious about tomorrow, for tomorrow will have worries and anxieties of its own. Sufficient for each day is its own trouble" (AMPC). In other words, Jesus is telling us not to spend today worrying about tomorrow. All of our todays have enough trouble—and we only have enough grace and enough energy to deal with today. Just as each day has its own trouble, each day has its own supply of grace. God does not give us grace today to live tomorrow. We need to make the most of the grace we have today, refuse to be anxious about tomorrow, determine to leave our prayers in God's hands, and not take our problems back by worrying about them.

God does not give us grace today
to live tomorrow.

6. NEGATIVE SPEECH

We can construct barriers to effective prayer and render our prayers ineffective with negative words. When we pray and then allow doubt and unbelief to take root in our minds and begin to speak negatively, we can hinder our prayers. When we pray and ask God to do something and then turn around and say, "I am afraid God will not come through for me," that is a negative confession.

· The words we speak are powerful, more powerful than we realize. In fact, Proverbs 18:21 says, "Death and life are in the power of the tongue, and they who indulge in it shall eat the fruit of it [for death or life]" (AMPC). In other words, we will have what we say, so we need to be speaking positively, not negatively. When we pray and ask God to do something and then turn around and say, "I'm afraid God won't come through for me," we are not speaking words of life.

Isaiah 53:7 says that Jesus was "oppressed and… afflicted, yet He opened not His mouth" (NKJV). I believe Jesus stayed silent because He knew that negative words could thwart or delay God's plan by speaking them at the wrong time. Certainly, His trials were difficult—unimaginably agonizing and grueling—but He did not complain.

What was true for Jesus during His most difficult hour needs to be true of us also. When we are going through hard times, let's commit to not opening our mouths in negative ways. Let's not complain, murmur, speak ill of others, or voice doubts about God with our words. You see, our words do not exist independently of who we are. Instead, our words represent who we are because they reveal what is in our hearts. Matthew 12:34 says, "For out of the abundance of the heart the mouth speaks" (NKJV). When our hearts are full of doubt, we will make negative confessions, but when they are filled with faith, our words will reveal our confidence and trust in God. When God hears a prayer followed by a negative confession, He does not respond. But when He hears a prayer that is accompanied by words that express confidence in Him, He delights to answer.

> *Our words represent who we are because they reveal what is in our hearts.*

7. LACK OF BOLDNESS

Many people feel hesitant to pray for various reasons. They may not think they know how to pray, they may be unsure of who God is, they may not be confident that God will hear their prayers, they may be intimidated because they view God as an angry Judge rather than a loving Father, or they may not believe God loves them enough to pay attention to their prayers and answer them. People lack boldness in prayer for many reasons, but regardless of why people don't approach God boldly, failing to do so is a barrier to effective prayer.

To pray powerful prayers, we need to pray boldly, meaning confidently and without fear or reservation. We can be bold enough to ask God for big things. We can approach God with boldness because Jesus has made us righteous (rightly related to God) through His death on the cross. Second Corinthians 5:21 says, "God made him who had no sin to be sin for us, so that in him we might become the righteousness of God."

Because of what Jesus has done for us, we can go to God with total confidence and pray unashamedly, knowing that He loves us, hears us, and will answer our prayers in the ways that are best for us.

When we understand that we can approach God with boldness, we will be able to overcome the enemy's attempts to make us feel condemned, and we will become daring in our prayers. We will no longer say to ourselves, *Well, I know God can do great things, but I find it hard to believe He will do them for me.* We think such thoughts because we do not think we are worthy, but we must always remember that Jesus has made us worthy. When we approach God boldly, we can count on Him to be merciful to us, according to Hebrews 4:16:

> Let us then fearlessly and confidently and boldly draw near to the throne of grace (the throne of God's unmerited favor to us sinners), that we may receive mercy [for our failures] and find grace to help in good time for every need [appropriate help and well-timed help, coming just when we need it]. (AMPC)

Mercy means that God will bless us when we do not deserve to be blessed—if we are bold enough to ask. We ask in Jesus' name, not in our own name. This means we are presenting to the Father all that Jesus is, not all that we are. We are nothing without Jesus!

When people ask me to do something for them, I respond better if they approach me with confidence than if they are timid or hesitant. I want them to be respectful and thankful but not fearful. Confidence breeds confidence. In other words, when people approach me with confidence, their confidence gives me confidence that they can handle what they ask for. However, if they come in fear or lacking boldness, I am hesitant to partner with them in anything, because where fear exists, the devil has an open door to bring defeat.

Ephesians 3:20 tells us that God is able to do more than we could ever dare to hope, ask, or think, so we need to determine to be daring and to avail ourselves of all He can do by asking boldly.

Don't ask God for less than you would like to. When a certain desire is in your heart, be bold in praying for it, if it is His will. Approach God with confidence, and ask Him for great things, and give Him a chance to show you just how great He really is.

> *Approach God with confidence.*

8. NOT RELATING PROPERLY TO AUTHORITY

Proverbs 28:9 makes a startling statement about what happens to our prayers when we are not properly related to the authority God has placed in our lives: "He who turns away his ear from hearing the law [of God and man], even his prayer is an abomination, hateful and revolting [to God]" (AMPC).

In many areas of life, someone is in a position of authority over another person or a group of people. And God is in authority over everyone. We deal with authority in our marriages, in our spiritual lives, in our professional lives, and even as citizens who are subject to traffic laws, taxes, and such simple messages as "Put Carts Here" in grocery store parking lots. As in any other realm in which authority is in place, being properly related to God's authority paves the way for us to experience answered prayer and His favor in our lives.

Just as being rightly related to authority is a key to powerful prayer, being rebellious toward authority will keep our prayers from being answered. We can see rebellion all around us in marriages and families, in schools, in workplaces, in civic settings, and on the street, so to speak. If we refuse to submit to earthly authority, then we will not submit to God's authority. In any area of a society where there is rebellion, there is dishonor and disobedience toward God because, according to Romans 13:1, "There is no authority except from God, and those that exist have been instituted by God" (ESV). This verse occurs in the context of governmental authority, but I believe we can apply it to many forms of authority.

We not only see rebellion and a lack of proper relating to authority in society; we also see that some people have trouble relating properly to spiritual authority. And Paul writes in 2 Corinthians 1:24, "Not that we have dominion [over you] and lord it over your faith, but [rather that we work with you as] fellow laborers [to promote] your joy" (AMPC). If we will understand and believe that spiritual authority exists to promote our joy, we will embrace it, and when we do, our joy will increase and our prayers will be powerful. I think it is easy to see that rebellion is increasing in the world today. Few people seem to want anyone telling them what to do. God gives authority for the sake of order, and rebellion is dangerous. In fact, based on 2 Thessalonians 2: 1–9, rebellion is related to the "man of lawlessness," whom scholars generally agree to be the Antichrist.

Many people would experience tremendous breakthroughs in prayer if they would simply stop being rebellious and learn to relate properly to authority. Remember, God puts authority in place in order to keep us safe and promote our joy. He gives us both spiritual authority and natural authority, and it is just as important to obey natural authority as it is to obey spiritual authority. Develop a God-honoring attitude toward every form of authority in your life, and make sure you are not rebellious in any way. I do want to say here that we do not have to obey authority if the person with the authority is telling us to do something that would be sinful, but neither should we have a rebellious attitude. Rebellion builds a barrier against answered prayer, but a proper relationship to authority makes a way for prayers to be powerful.

> *God puts authority in place in order*
> *to keep us safe and promote our joy.*

Conclusion

I sincerely hope that this book has helped you grow in your relationship with God through prayer and that you have learned some lessons that have set you free from any misconceptions you may have had about prayer in the past. I hope you've realized that prayer is much easier than you may have thought and that it doesn't have to be long, complicated, or eloquent to be powerful—nor do you have to be perfect. You can pray anywhere, anytime. No subject is off-limits. God cares about everything you care about because He cares so much about *you*.

In this book, you've read about the habits of people who pray powerful prayers, and I want you to know that few people develop these habits overnight. They take time, but as you stay committed to them, you will grow in them. The same is true for breaking through the barriers to effective prayer. You may not break through all of them in a week, but now that you are aware of them, you can work on them for as long as it takes to eliminate them from your life.

You may remember that I wrote early in the book about asking God to teach you to pray. Prayer is not a one-time lesson but a relationship that deepens as you walk with God throughout your life. I encourage you to *keep asking* Him to teach you to pray, because all of us can always increase in spiritual maturity and in intimacy with God. Ask Him to help you grow in prayer, to help you pray more powerfully, or to guide you when you aren't sure how to pray about specific situations or for certain people.

I am praying for you—that your relationship with God will become more intimate, more fulfilling, and more powerful as He continues to teach you to pray and as you enjoy a rich and rewarding walk with Him through prayer.

Notes

1   Andrew Murray, *With Christ in the School of Prayer* (New York: Fleming H. Revell, 1895), 5–6.

2   Jeanne Guyon, *Experiencing the Depths of Jesus Christ* (Beaumont, TX: SeedSowers, 1975), 64.

3   Charles Spurgeon, "Prayer Certified of Success," *Metropolitan Tabernacle Pulpit*, vol. 19, January 19, 1873, https://www.spurgeon.org/resource-library/sermons /prayer-certified-of-success.

SOURCE NOTES

Do you have a real relationship with Jesus?

God loves you! He created you to be a special, unique, one-of-a-kind individual, and He has a specific purpose and plan for your life. And through a personal relationship with your Creator—God—you can discover a way of life that will truly satisfy your soul.

No matter who you are, what you've done, or where you are in your life right now, God's love and grace are greater than your sin—your mistakes. Jesus willingly gave His life so you can receive forgiveness from God and have new life in Him. He's just waiting for you to invite Him to be your Savior and Lord.

If you are ready to commit your life to Jesus and follow Him, all you have to do is ask Him to forgive your sins and give you a fresh start in the life you are meant to live. Begin by praying this prayer . . .

Lord Jesus, thank You for giving Your life
for me and forgiving me of my sins so I can have
a personal relationship with You. I am sincerely
sorry for the mistakes I've made, and I know
I need You to help me live right.

*Your Word says in Romans 10:9, "If you declare
with your mouth, 'Jesus is Lord,' and believe in
your heart that God raised him from the dead,
you will be saved" (NIV). I believe You are the Son
of God and confess You as my Savior and Lord.
Take me just as I am, and work in my heart,
making me the person You want me to be.
I want to live for You, Jesus, and I am so grateful
that You are giving me a fresh start in my
new life with You today.
I love You, Jesus!*

It's so amazing to know that God loves us so much! He
wants to have a deep, intimate relationship with us that
grows every day as we spend time with Him in prayer
and Bible study. And we want to encourage you in your
new life in Christ.

Please visit joycemeyer.org/salvation to request Joyce's
book *A New Way of Living*, which is our gift to you. We
also have other free resources online to help you make
progress in pursuing everything God has for you.
Congratulations on your fresh start in your life in Christ!
We hope to hear from you soon.

About the Author

Joyce Meyer is one of the world's leading practical Bible teachers and a *New York Times* bestselling author. Joyce's books have helped millions of people find hope and restoration through Jesus Christ. Joyce's program, *Enjoying Everyday Life*, is broadcast on television, radio, and online to millions worldwide in over one hundred languages.

Through Joyce Meyer Ministries, Joyce teaches internationally on a number of topics with a particular focus on how the Word of God applies to our everyday lives. Her candid communication style allows her to share openly and practically about her experiences so others can apply what she has learned to their lives.

Joyce has authored more than 140 books, which have been translated into more than 160 languages, and over 39 million of her books have been distributed worldwide. Bestsellers include *Power Thoughts*; *The Confident Woman*; *Look Great, Feel Great*; *Starting*

Your Day Right; *Ending Your Day Right*; *Approval Addiction*; *How to Hear from God*; *Beauty for Ashes*; and *Battlefield of the Mind*.

Joyce's passion to help people who are hurting is foundational to the vision of Hand of Hope, the missions arm of Joyce Meyer Ministries. Each year Hand of Hope provides millions of meals for the hungry and malnourished, installs freshwater wells in poor and remote areas, provides critical relief after natural disasters, and offers free medical and dental care to thousands through their hospitals and clinics worldwide. Through Project GRL, women and children are rescued from human trafficking and provided safe places to receive an education, nutritious meals, and the love of God.

JOYCE MEYER MINISTRIES

U.S. & FOREIGN OFFICE ADDRESSES

Joyce Meyer Ministries
P.O. Box 655
Fenton, MO 63026
USA
(636) 349-0303

Joyce Meyer Ministries—Canada
P.O. Box 7700
Vancouver, BC V6B 4E2
Canada
(800) 868-1002

Joyce Meyer Ministries—Australia
Locked Bag 77
Mansfield Delivery Centre
Queensland 4122
Australia
(07) 3349 1200

Joyce Meyer Ministries—England
P.O. Box 1549
Windsor SL4 1GT
United Kingdom
01753 831102

Joyce Meyer Ministries—South Africa
P.O. Box 5
Cape Town 8000
South Africa
(27) 21-701-1056

Joyce Meyer Ministries—Francophonie
29 avenue Maurice Chevalier
77330 Ozoir la Ferriere
France

Joyce Meyer Ministries—Germany
Postfach 761001
22060 Hamburg
Germany
+49 (0)40 / 88 88 4 11 11

Joyce Meyer Ministries—Netherlands
Lorenzlaan 14
7002 HB Doetinchem
+31 657 555 9789

Joyce Meyer Ministries—Russia
P.O. Box 789
Moscow 101000
Russia
+7 (495) 727-14-68

OTHER BOOKS BY JOYCE MEYER

Teenagers Are People Too!
Trusting God Day by Day
The Word, the Name, the Blood
Woman to Woman
You Can Begin Again
*Your Battles Belong to the Lord**

Joyce Meyer Spanish Titles

Auténtica y única
(Authentically, Uniquely You)
Belleza en lugar de cenizas
(Beauty for Ashes)
Buena salud, buena vida
(Good Health, Good Life)
Cambia tus palabras, cambia tu vida
(Change Your Words, Change Your Life)
El campo de batalla de la mente
(Battlefield of the Mind)
Cómo envejecer sin avejentarse
(How to Age without Getting Old)
Como formar buenos habitos y romper malos habitos
(Making Good Habits, Breaking Bad Habits)
La conexión de la mente
(The Mind Connection)
Dios no está enojado contigo
(God Is Not Mad at You)
La dosis de aprobación
(The Approval Fix)
Efesios: Comentario biblico
(Ephesians: Biblical Commentary)

Empezando tu día bien
(Starting Your Day Right)
Hágalo con miedo
(Do It Afraid)
Hazte un favor a ti mismo…perdona
(Do Yourself a Favor…Forgive)
Madre segura de sí misma
(The Confident Mom)
Momentos de quietud con Dios
(Quiet Times with God Devotional)
Mujer segura de sí misma
(The Confident Woman)
No se afane por nada
(Be Anxious for Nothing)
Pensamientos de poder
(Power Thoughts)
Sanidad para el alma de una mujer
(Healing the Soul of a Woman)
Sanidad para el alma de una mujer, devocionario
(Healing the Soul of a Woman Devotional)
Santiago: Comentario bíblico
(James: Biblical Commentary)
Sobrecarga
(Overload)*
Sus batallas son del Señor
(Your Battles Belong to the Lord)
Termina bien tu día
(Ending Your Day Right)
Tienes que atreverte
(I Dare You)

Usted puede comenzar de nuevo
(You Can Begin Again)
Viva amando su vida
(Living a Life You Love)
Viva valientemente
(Living Courageously)
Vive por encima de tus sentimientos
(Living beyond Your Feelings)

* Study Guide available for this title

Books by Dave Meyer
Life Lines